VOCATIONS AND THEIR FORMATION TODAY

Visit our web site at
www.albahouse.org
(for orders www.stpauls.us)

or call 1-800-343-2522 (ALBA)
and request current catalog

VOCATIONS AND THEIR FORMATION TODAY

FORMATION IN THE RELIGIOUS LIFE
Call, Discernment, Adaptation

GUY LESPINAY, O.P.

ST PAULS

First published in Canada in 2002 by Médiaspaul under the title
Être Formateur Aujourd'hui : La formation à la vie religieuse.

Library of Congress Cataloging-in-Publication Data

Lespinay, Guy.
  [Être formateur aujourd'hui. English]
  Vocations and their formation today: formation in the religious life, call, discernment,
adaptation / Guy Lespinay.
    p. cm.
  Includes bibliographical references and index.
  ISBN 13: 978-0-8189-1307-5
  ISBN 10: 0-8189-1307-X
  1. Vocation (in religious orders, congregations, etc.) 2. Vocation—Catholic Church.
3. Happiness—Religious aspects—Catholic Church. 4. Self-realization—Religious
aspects—Catholic Church. I. Title.
  BX2435.L4813 2010
  248.8'94—dc22

2009028287

Produced and designed in the United States of America by the
Fathers and Brothers of the Society of St. Paul,
2187 Victory Boulevard, Staten Island, New York 10314-6603
as part of their communications apostolate.

ISBN 10: 0-8189-1307-X
ISBN 13: 978-0-8189-1307-5

Printing Information:

Current Printing - first digit	1	2	3	4	5	6	7	8	9	10

Year of Current Printing - first year shown

2009	2010	2011	2012	2013	2014	2015	2016	2017	2018

TABLE OF CONTENTS

Preface xi

Foreword xv
  The "How" or the "Why" of Religious Life xvi
  Discernment in the Face of Positive and
    Negative Experiences xix
  Are Aptitudes Signs? xxiv
  Attitudes of Those Responsible for Formation xxv
  Certainty and Religious Life xxvi

Acknowledgments xxix

Chapter 1: The Call to Religious Life 1
  From Whom Does the Call Come? 1
  The Mysterious Character of the Call 2
  God Calls by Means of the Events of One's Life 4
  The Basis of our Choices 5
  The Birth of a Desire 7
  Time for Thinking Things Over 8
  How to Discover the Call via Aspirations 9
  The Desire To Meet God and Set Out;
    an Exodus Spirituality 10

Chapter 2: The Signs Accompanying the Choice
    of Religious Life 19
  What is Discernment? 19
  Who is to Discern? 20
  Choosing on the Basis of Desires and Motivations 21

The Desire to Encounter God
   A God Who Makes Sense of My Life 22
The Desire to Live in a Group 25
The Desire for a Change in Life, Conversion 30
The Desire to Follow Jesus 34
Trust in the Future 35
Renunciation 37
The Taste for Knowing and Learning 38
Generosity 39
The Quest for an Institutional Form of Life 40
Conclusion 42

Chapter 3: Who Are the Young Today? 43
A First Statement 43
The Universe of the Young 44
Values That Can Favor a Call to Religious Life 47
What Are Young People Expecting from Us? 49
Their Apprehensions 52
The Fear of Commitment 54
The Fear of Rules 56
Some Reference Points for Formation 57

Chapter 4: Accompanying Vocations 61
Motivations 61
Elitism in Religious Life 63
The Exercise of Compassion: Truth or Ideology 65
The Candidate's Personal Background 69
Vital Strengths of the Individual 70
Purity of Intentions and Commitments 73

Chapter 5: Pre-Formation 75
To Be Successful: A Gradual Entering 75
The Family Background 77
Pastoral Aptitudes or Psychotherapy 78
The Pre-formation Steps 81

Chapter 6: Adaptation to Religious Life 89
A New Phase: The Formation Itself 89

Table of Contents

Entry into Religious Life.. 91

First Challenges 98

Emotional life and sexuality 121

Conclusion 127

Chapter 7: Persons in Charge of Formation and
            of the Community of Formation 129

Introduction 129

The ideal community 130

A shared responsibility.. 132

Who has to adapt? 133

The person in charge of formation.................................... 136

The relation between the person in charge
    of formation and the person in formation 140

Religious culture... 142

Psychological accompaniment 143

Training those in charge of formation................................143

Hopes and fears 144

Conclusion 147

Chapter 8: Evaluation 149

Introduction 149

Some general considerations 149

The candidate in formation 151

The evaluation report to the community and the council......154

An evaluation of the programs...157

Chapter 9: Pastoral Work with Vocations...........................159

The Mysterious Choices of God Exerted on Men 159

Developing a Positive Attitude towards our Way of Life 161

A visible community...163

An open community...165

Praying Communities...167

Take time to live 168

Conclusion 169

Bibliography 171

Endnotes...173

PREFACE

Formation in religious life today is not an easy subject to deal with. It is a very complex matter; indeed, it has become even more so since we live in a time of doubt and uncertainty, when religious houses are closing and more than a few religious communities are facing the possibility of extinction for lack of vocations. Yet, while it is neither popular, nor easy to speak positively of religious life, and much less of formation for religious life, we must find the courage to do so!

Friar Guy Lespinay, born in Canada, spent many years in France as the Formation Director of the Dominican students there. This has afforded him the rare opportunity to compare and consider the different situations in formation existing both in his native Canada and abroad. As he mentions in his book, Friar Guy was a latecomer to the Dominican Order. Although this text does not allow the reader the possibility of appreciating either the warmth of his voice or his accent, so well imitated by former students, one can yet sense the solid human experience which imparts depth and soundness to his reflections. Friar Guy, in laying out the conditions for a genuine welcoming process, which fully respects the discernment and frailty of incoming persons, notes clearly that "when we rush into things, people can get burnt."

He sets out a number of priorities and responsibilities in which the first person responsible for discernment is the candidate himself. Such an observation, while apparently obvious, deserves emphasis. That a candidate feels called to the religious life already indicates a desire to seek God. Such a desire, though, needs to be met with prayer in community, and to be clothed in the signs of that encounter with God which marks the consecrated life. Young people expect in their elders an authenticity to equal their own idealism. In this, however, their individuality and autonomy must be respected, both at the level of thought (if they are not to become the hostages of an ideology) and emotions, because those in charge of their formation must not attempt to coerce them into a commitment to, or to a love for the religious life.

Friar Guy remarks that often formation in religious life has encouraged a certain regression to an adolescent or even childish developmental stage. As an antidote to this, he suggests trust, given without hesitation. For this reason, he believes that it is essential to assign responsibilities early on to young religious.

The formation plan has to be clear, since one cannot adapt to what one does not know. Yet, in its clarity, the plan must not become too rigid. "If a man had to say yes to a lifestyle amounting to nothing more than to existing in a static situation, he might as well bury himself alive." He stresses the importance of finding a rhythm in formation, quite aware that spirituality has to be put into perspective so as to avoid the tendency to stagnate on the one hand, or to romanticize on the other, as both extremes miss the concrete demands of pedagogical experience. "One must not hurry young plants into blooming," said another Father Master. The deeper the movement, the slower it is. One must be patient, for we are dealing here with a work of conversion.

This book will consider in turn the differences between

monasteries and apostolic congregations, without devoting special chapters to each type of community. Rather, the author focuses a remark here and there, for example, on the difficulties met in contemplative monasteries where the number of young people in formation are few and formation can last six or eight years without a change of spiritual guide.

This book is extremely interesting for the way in which it draws our attention to details frequently assumed (and thus often forgotten), while at the same time considering the young candidate to religious life as representative of his generation. The author emphasizes the fact that those wishing to enter are not yet accustomed to the demands of living a community life, or to what was once termed asceticism (a word never employed by the author!). The work also points out a number of the snares into which formation communities may fall, for example, harshly critiquing the candidate, or alternately, using those in formation as household servants. These are all pitfalls that are easily and best avoided!

In short, this is a straightforward, solid, and faithful book that avoids indulging in illusions and outlines the conditions for a genuine journey of conversion. Hence it may well be of interest to the laity as well!

Friar Michel Van Aerde, O.P.
Provincial Prior of the Dominican Province of Toulouse

FOREWORD

I have taken up the question of formation to religious life in this book as the direct result of my experiences as a spiritual guide in contact with a large number of young people, and in response to a number of requests urging me to put my thoughts into writing. Through this process, I have come to realize that oftentimes those in charge of formation may feel uneasy faced with the task of forming young candidates. A number of communities have contacted me requesting my input on a particular situation, or to ask a question on how best to handle a certain matter. It seems to me that, while there are workshops and sessions offered to prepare these individuals, experience is still the best guide. It is this experience which I set out to share in this book.

Over the years I have received many requests for my lecture-notes on formation. With this book, I am making them available as fully and widely as I can. My thoughts here reflect in writing what a long pastoral experience with young people has taught me. However, much remains to be done to explore the matter in depth. For the time being, I have left aside the psychological aspect of problems, which are, in truth, better dealt with by professionals in that field. Thus, while my work cannot be thought of as the definitive and conclusive work on the subject, still, coupled with a reading of a variety of other authors, one may come to a better understanding of just how complex a vocation is.

Whatever we might say and do on our part to discern a vocation, forming an individual for religious life will always fall short of what God's grace can accomplish with anyone who wishes to follow Christ. No theory, ideology or general notion on the subject can replace prayerful discernment and good will in counseling candidates. The future of religious life should not revolve around lofty ideals beyond the capacity of today's young person to reach. Instead, the one in charge of formation, and the community collaborating with him, must adapt and respond to the difficulties encountered by those who are in formation. Everything must be lived out as an act of faith and mercy towards all those whom the Lord sends our way. Let us be wary of making simplistic judgments of others and, thereby, end up relying too much upon our own personal behavior as a guide. Let us rather allow grace to work through the process, and prevent our discussion about religious life from becoming dogmatic! It is possible that we become too sure of ourselves; so, let us approach the theme with care and prudence.

The "How" or the "Why" of Religious Life

The purpose of the *exposé* I gave to the superiors of religious communities and to those in charge of formation was not really to justify the "*why?*" of religious life, or, for that matter, to explain its theological mysteries, or even to propose a spirituality of the religious life. Numerous studies in recent years have dealt with the theological aspects of consecrated life, stressing service in and for the Church. Such reflection has brought about major changes in our lifestyle and our vision about the future of religious life. It seems that what is lacking now is the "*how*" of formation rather than the "*why*." Therefore, I will not attempt here to justify the existence of the consecrated life, but rather to speak of the key questions and difficulties that arise during the period of formation while examining the attitudes and methods surrounding the integration of new generations into religious communities.

Essentially, religious life is a means towards an end, and not an end in itself. It ought to lead to personal happiness and correspond to the desire of those who wish to embark upon this journey. For any individual, time is required to attain an emotional equilibrium, moving beyond formalism, yet avoiding sinking into unbridled license. All of us who are members of religious communities must develop a deep sense of moral accountability to God, who has called us to such a great vocation. Christian communities make a great number of demands on those who proclaim themselves to be witnesses of God's intervention and His action in the world. We must be conscious of this and get prepared for it.

A Christian is called to holiness and accomplishes his mission in and for the Church in service to humanity. There can be no question about this. He does so finding God through the love of his wife and children. Loving them brings him to a fuller understanding of God's love.

Religious live out the universal call to holiness, but differently. For them, it begins with a public commitment, whereby they consecrate their life totally to the Lord. It is through God that he or she really rediscovers the divine hand at work in others and comes to love them because of that. A religious is not a privileged functionary, adept at any task, geared only to service in an institution, whether that institution be the Church or any other organization in which he might be involved. A religious is primarily a sign of God's goodness to the world. He or she evangelizes the world in a contemplative way. A community of brothers or sisters, then, has an ecclesial character, as it manifests God's presence in humanity.

Is not the repugnance felt towards institutions by Christians today, and above all by young people, caused by a utilitarian mentality often manifested by those engaged in the service of the Church, by local governments, or sometimes by those responsible for future priestly and religious vocations? In one of his lectures, Cardinal Ratzinger said: "*We talk too much about the Church and not enough about God.*" I quite agree.

Wittingly or unwittingly, one enters religious life to find happiness by searching for God and wishing to do so within a community. According to Saint Thomas Aquinas, any state of life corresponds to a person's desire to be happy. Saint Thomas goes on to note: "*Effectively, charity has two great precepts: one concerns the love of God, the other the love of one's neighbor.*" These two precepts are connected to one another by charity. Accordingly, what we must love in charity above all else, is the supreme good, namely, God. It is this fundamental attachment to God that makes us happy. In a secondary position and flowing from it, is the love, in charity, that we must show to our neighbor. Such an understanding entails a certain social or communal quality to our participation in everlasting happiness, which we will share with others.[1] Religious life builds on the principle that everyone seeks happiness. A religious finds it by living his or her baptismal vocation through a commitment to the vows and life in a community. This way of living out one's baptismal vocation should lead to happiness.

Thus, we see how important the "how" is for choosing the consecrated life. While the "*why?*" – which may be expressed as a need for service – is not a cause sufficient to lead to the renunciation entailed by religious life. In fact, consciousness of the Church's ecclesial and missionary character often comes much later. Inclination to missionary work for some individuals may justify the decision to enter, but, in essence, that decision remains marked by the desire for self-fulfillment and happiness. By itself, the missionary inclination will not, in the long run, guarantee perseverance. For once disappointments take their toll, a religious can easily become disillusioned. Such setbacks can only be overcome by a close relationship with God who urges the religious to serve and glorify Him in happiness.

Discernment in the Face of Positive and Negative Experiences

If an individual hopes to arrive at some sort of meaningful decision, discerning a vocation cannot be based solely on his or her previous negative experiences. Of course, negative past experiences are important and deserve consideration, since they influence our lives. Yet, negative experiences in themselves should help us build our future and prepare us to live moments of joy and gladness, not the other way around. A candidate's past is significant, but the future must also be built on positive elements since these elements, too, are part of one's own personal history.

As those in charge of formation, priors, or novice masters, it is likely that we have a lot of experience; *"I've been there before!"* we might say to ourselves. Do be careful, though. If somebody comes to us with only negative experiences, that person will end up with negative attitudes towards himself and those he lives with. The same applies to us as their guides. The more we are influenced by our apprehensions, the more we convey them to others. If we form a negative climate within and around us, we will impart our apprehensions and our anxiety to others. Perhaps if we start out by discovering the positive experiences, the result will be, by far, more gratifying. In the Lord's vineyard there is no room for pessimism. We are saved by the love of God. Consequently, we must portray an attitude of compassion and mercy, conveying this love and goodness to others.

Aspirants coming to us to discover religious life want to be accompanied in their quest. They do not come, though, in order to take on our problems and hang-ups. Consciously or not, they are seeking God! For the moment, the Benedictines, the Cistercians, the Carmelites, as well as some new religious communities are very popular because they project this image of people searching for God. That is what people are longing for, sometimes even to the extent of gravitating around religious sects. This search for God is the main characteristic of all religious. How many Dominican friars have said: "*I had a contemplative life in mind, but I wanted to preach and to be a missionary.*" They ended up opting for some order or congregation more in resonance with their apostolic aspirations. Our own apostolic communities, Dominican or otherwise, insist a great deal on missionary activities. That is certainly important. However, the search for happiness is more important yet, and this can be found only in a relationship with God. This may be the reason for the many converts wishing to join our communities.

Is it possible that, by our sometimes suspicious attitudes, we are attempting to turn the religious life into a sort of club of perfect intellectuals, expert in divine realities, holy and virtuous performers, and skilful arbitrators of moral issues for our fellow human beings? If so, very few people will develop the skills required for religious life, or be motivated by it. Should not religious life be a way of helping the world to find God? I think so. Such a vocation is a challenge, though, and one that should give us cause for concern, especially those of us called to assist others in discerning their vocation, or to enhance their adaptation to community life.

A theology that views religious life as superior to other vocations, stresses the excellence of its members as the main goal. Yet, this is a manner of misrepresenting the purpose of any consecration to God. It is a deep humility, rather than a sense of our excellence, which must characterize our life from the outset, and which must inspire a degree of detachment from our views and ideals. It is not uncommon that after a number of years in religious life, we may accumulate a number of determined and very passionate views about the particulars of our way of life. However, those who wish to follow Christ in what is for them a new way, have not yet reached that point. Let us, therefore, be a bit more modest in our determinations, so as to move forward at the same pace as the candidates who come to us.

If memory serves me well, there are eleven degrees of humility in the *Spiritual Conferences* of John Cassian, and twelve degrees in the *Rule of Saint Benedict*. It is this profound humility so characteristic of early monastic traditions that must mark the religious vocation. In the time of Bishop Foulques, in the 13th Century, people used to call the Toulouse preachers (i.e., the Dominicans) "the humble friars." That is because the journey of the Preachers (and of all religious) must be one of humility. It is not an easy road. It involves constant self-abnegation and renunciation.

To become a guide in the religious life, two very important qualities are required: humility and a sense of humor. Without them, one cannot effectively promote vocations within a community. If we take matters too seriously and expect religious to be perfect performers, we will easily eliminate many aspirants. My impression is that we have to do some soul-searching and humbly recognize that we are limited human beings. Through recognition of our own poverty, though, we will be better able to extend a welcoming hand to a candidate. Let us be careful! Too much confidence in our own wisdom could cause our downfall.

Every person is unique. Many learning experiences have brought us to this point in our life. Each person is a treasure in whom the Holy Spirit has chosen to make his dwelling. Yet, those who come our way may surprise us. Friar Timothy Radcliffe, former Master of the Order of Preachers (Dominicans), talks about a God who upsets us because He shows up at the door in company with His pals; and these friends of His are not always those to whom we would like to open our door. The friends Jesus brings our way are more or less interesting. At any rate, they are the ones He has summoned. When God comes to visit us, He doesn't come alone and He asks us to broaden our living space. Timothy Radcliffe says:

> A century or so ago, the English upper-classes used to tremble when getting a letter from the King or Queen announcing the royal wish to visit their home. Lodging the royals in a guest room was out of the question. Generally one had to demolish half the house, build some twenty extra rooms and install special rest rooms. One hostess had her home entirely rebuilt to receive His Majesty; when she asked him if everything was to his liking, he majestically replied: "Madam, I'd appreciate a hook in the washroom on which to hang my housecoat." Imagine what it means for the whole Blessed Trinity to switch lodgings, as it were, and take up residence in our souls. The first consequence is to oust doors and windows, at once opening up

our cramped quarters. Every religious community, congregation, province or monastery is a tiny space which welcomes some people, excludes others, and makes some feel at ease, others not at ease. The doors are opened to some, closed to others; but when God takes up His dwelling in us, cramped quarters expand to make room for God and all God's friends. God did say to Isaiah: "Enlarge your tent's size and layout without stinting the covers that shelter you, stretch out the ropes, and reinforce the stakes." God requires a vast place.[2]

Was religious life instituted only to welcome a certain category of persons, the ones well balanced from the outset, having within themselves the prospect of forming the future elite in our religious communities or in the Church? I think this is a fundamental question in the debate on vocations to the religious life. What is the aim of religious life? To whom is it addressed? We have never had so many tools to help us discern serious vocations, and yet, we keep seeing religious leaving their communities after final vows for all sorts of reasons.

A vocation is a call that comes from God. I intend to keep that in mind throughout my reflections. Since God is calling us, we have to discern the signs of that call with much caution and simplicity. Are we sufficiently detached to discern whether or not God is calling? Are we sure we are not mistaken? Do we really know what God wants? Only He can read minds. Let us try to focus on certain aptitudes amidst the multiplicity of signs. Now, the individual may very well feel he has a call. That is something we have to respect. I rarely tell anyone that he does, or does not, have a vocation. I prefer to find out what makes him happy. From there we can go forward.

Are Aptitudes Signs?

Along with the candidates themselves we can discover signs indicating possibilities for personal growth. Some aptitudes are required. But most of them are innate tendencies slowly developed and solidified with time.

Above all we have to work on the predispositions necessary to succeed in this vocation. That is how we prepare for the future. We have a tendency to classify people according to categories, and consequently, to determine whether or not they have a vocation. Maybe we function too much like inspectors conducting investigations; thus, we neglect our role to accompany the individual on his or her journey. Religious life is indeed a journey one embarks upon with God and one's community. We ought not wager on the capacities of each candidate.

It is often said that the call comes from God! Then, if this is the case, we have a responsibility vis-à-vis God and vis-à-vis those He calls, i.e., with respect to human and Christian communities. At certain points in time, in the Church, the invitation came from the promoter of vocations, the master of novices, or the director of the seminar! Resorting to psychological assessment today may be useful and even necessary but I personally don't waste time sending potential friars to therapy. In this, for me, there is no wavering whatsoever. What determines a call is not psychology. It is just one of the many ways to discover the call. On the other hand, I know of religious communities that have been destroyed by group therapy. The purpose of religious life is not to conduct guinea-pig experiments. The life of a religious is a road along which one strives to achieve holiness, or rather, strives to let oneself be sanctified. And that is no easy task! The essential foundation for "becoming" holy is humility. It takes years to get there. Those in charge of formation cannot do without it. I prefer an individual who is less competent, but aware of his limitations and weak points, to one who knows it all but is ignorant when it comes to himself.

Attitudes of Those Responsible for Formation

I am sometimes astonished by the attitudes of religious towards newcomers. We conduct an analysis of young candidates; we describe their difficulties in numerous detail, the shortcomings in their education, their insecurities, or their detectable psychological problems. However, to work in the field of formation nowadays, a person must cleanse his mind of predetermined notions, and that is difficult! We must set aside our expectations, fears, frustrations, and look objectively to find what is genuine and great in the person who wants to join us. Does the individual want to consecrate himself to God? Does he want to get closer to Him? "Same old story," you will say! Yet, that is precisely the reason for which one should enter religious life. For mission or our apostolate can be accomplished by any other individual wishing to follow Christ and work in His vineyard. Our aspirants must seek to walk in Christ's footsteps according to a particular charism. It is this charism that will help him or her to blossom.

After assessing such willingness on the potential candidate's part, we can pass on to the next step. This involves helping the person to develop the necessary aptitudes to fulfill his or her deep inner desire. This is the phase for the discernment of a vocation, preparing the person to live the proposed ideal.

Certainty and Religious Life

We must not hope for irreproachable conduct from those entering our communities, expecting them to demonstrate the same maturity of someone already twenty or fifty years in the religious life. Moreover, at what age does one become perfect? We must not expect the candidate to be well-versed in religious matters, measured by our own yardstick.

Life is an apprenticeship during which we walk along our own way of the Cross. What we are as novices is not necessarily what we will be in later life. Ask anyone who entered the religious life in the fifties or sixties, or later, and then left. It was often the most pious novices who broke ranks. I have the impression that sometimes the holier they were in the novitiate; the less they had the gift of perseverance, as strange as it may seem! I think of people who held important functions in their institutes. One day they wake up and radically alter the direction of their lives. What happened? No one knows. Such is the mystery of life. Others who were real "delinquents" in the religious life did persevere. Some even became highly esteemed Superiors. All this should make us feel dubious about our certainties. We must not over idealize our past. Let us not judge lightly. If a candidate has major problems, we simply have to refuse to allow him or her to go any further. Apart from such individuals, let us give others their chance and work with them so that they really discover their call. The friar who welcomed me into the novitiate – and he was an experienced Preacher – later told me [after I had spent nineteen years in religious life]: *"I didn't believe you had a vocation. I kept telling myself you were not made for us."* And yet others, who were younger and better prepared, didn't make the grade; they've gone back to the world, or they live on the perimeters of the community.

I like to think that we are an association of sinners. It is about time we realized that. We will get candidates when we become fully aware of the mystery dwelling within us. We are not here to welcome incoming saints. We are here to accept people who want to become saints. There may very well be criteria or conditions (for the acceptance of candidates to the religious life) at the intellectual and human levels, which we have to consider, but what would happen if we only accepted those who offer the best guarantees? A too demanding screening process could end up endangering the future of religious life.

Our great saints were always humble enough to recognize that they were sinners. They had both feet on the ground. Let us admit we do not know it all! Ultimately, God is the one who really forms us. Let us recognize that it is the Truth we must seek in everything, with mercy.

We must not harbor any illusion about the guarantees formation may provide. It is impossible to predict what will happen to somebody in the long run. There are so many factors to take into account.

Maybe we are too sure of ourselves! Humility, at least, helps us to progress more quickly toward a kind of wisdom of the heart. Give yourself the gift of charity. Strive to do good but let the Holy Spirit do the rest. Then you will see how much happier you will be. Confidence will grow insofar as you humbly entrust yourself to the Spirit of the Lord. Let grace work in you. Allow God to guide you. Put your trust in God, yourself, and above all, in others. And if you are full of faults and defects, give thanks to God. Perhaps that is what will make you an excellent spiritual guide for others. Your heart is what counts.

ACKNOWLEDGMENTS

The present work is the result of many lectures and sessions, as well as extensive experience with young people over a long period of time. However, it would never have seen the light of day without the collaboration of a great many people.

My gratitude goes first of all to the Dominican nuns of Lourdes for encouraging me in this work. It was they who taped the lectures, transformed them into a readable text and proofread the first drafts: Sister Isabel Marie, Prioress; Sister Anne Dominique and Sister Marie Veronique.

The French edition, too, was an enriching and communal experience, particularly when it came to the revisions of content and style. I wish to offer special thanks to Mrs. Joelle Marchand and her patient husband who assisted her in formatting the final text.

My gratitude extends especially to Mr. Lucien Forgues for his singular collaboration with the final presentation of the work and its final corrections.

Thanks also to Brother Jacques Bellemare for his competent translation of this work into English.

To everyone and all, I express my most sincere gratitude. A special thanks to Brother John Fitzgerald, F.C. who made the final corrections to the English text.

Brother Guy Lespinay, O.P.

VOCATIONS AND THEIR FORMATION TODAY

CHAPTER ONE

THE CALL TO RELIGIOUS LIFE

From Whom Does the Call Come?

Scripture attests that, historically, God calls people through the events of their lives. This call is always very personal. How often do young students or persons on a spiritual quest say: "How can I tell what God is calling me to? How do I know the will of God?" How can we respond to such sincerity?

The call does come from God. It is something that we proclaim everywhere. Too often, though, this way of speaking does not convey any meaning to the person in the street. There is little clarity in this matter. At first sight, neither the question nor the answer is crystal clear.

If the call does come from God, are not young people correct if they are amazed? God has never told them in clear terms what their vocation is. No evident sign seems to point to the way. In the Old Testament, God speaks to Moses, to a people, to prophets, even to kings, urging them to turn to a new way of life, to conversion. In Sacred Scripture we meet with visions, angels, and messengers; then there are dreams and voices. What about now? Who shows up to impart some message from God, to speak a word to young people today? How are they engaged? Still, we keep insisting that "God does call them."

And it is true! God does call them! But just how does He call them? We shall see in the first stage of our study.

The Mysterious Character of the Call

In 1970, Claude Geffré expressed clearly what must be understood by "a God who speaks to us":

> God speaks to people to this very day, but only in parables. But why, if God is our sole happiness, does He not speak more clearly? Why does He not force Himself on our attention? Here we meet with one of the most mysterious laws governing God's encounter with man. The fact that God's word has a veiled character – which troubles us – is really inseparable from His love, a requirement of the friendly dialogue He wants to have with each one of us individually.
>
> If the word of God were not veiled, it would no longer be the word of God: it would be one truth among many, a truth we could explore without changing our life, without conversion. If the word of God were to force itself upon us, it would not respect our freedom; it would not stimulate a loving response. God's word is both the revelation and the gift of a person which can only be accepted lovingly.
>
> God is all powerful but hides himself because it is a joy to Him to be loved freely by His creatures: He wants to be wanted.[3]

I am very fond of this commentary. It speaks to us about a preferential love and about encountering a person. It is through the events of life that we slowly discover love's demands. In the conversation of two people in love, there are always unknown areas. One party does not always say what he or she is, nor conveys what he or she feels. Their interior universe remains shrouded in mystery. After many years of intimacy, lovers still recognize that their secrets have not all been revealed. The moment they stop trying to unveil such secrets (which make for their uniqueness) there is no longer anything new and dynamic in their loving relationship.

God remains invisible and withdrawn. The first call we receive is intuitive, and may come as a surprise. We slowly have to discover those hidden nooks and crannies where God loves us in a more special way than usual, disclosing His presence and love. A person is unceasingly being renewed by the creative power of God: just consider the general call which is at the foundation of our Christian engagement. It is a call based on faith in God who loves us and can do everything out of love for us. Most of all, He wants us to be completely His. Anyone who opts for marriage is choosing a love that is shared. Anyone going in for religious life is making the choice of a love which is exclusive: the love of God alone. The person interested in finding out what his or her vocation is must probe into their interior world to discover whether they love enough to dedicate themselves to searching for that little secret corner that God keeps in store for them. It is not something forthcoming in an interview or a conversation, but only through a slow and profound communication process between the spiritual guide and the aspirant. What's more, nothing is certain; for it is God who offers Himself, and only the person called and his God are in possession of this mystery. Ambiguous signs are involved which may lead to judgmental errors about the individual who is being called.

God Calls by Means of the Events of One's Life

God calls us through the events of our lives, as He did in the past with the people of Israel. By intuition we slowly learn to make sense of our past. Faith helps us to discover the meaning of our existence. Intuition, in combination with events of significance and enlightened by faith, indicates if a call is ours. The vocation does not take root until this more or less clear call corresponds to a desire. That is how God's will takes shape and becomes noticeable. It is only after acting on this intuitive desire that we take stock of the call received; only then does an aspiration become a solid reality making us certain that we have made the right choice. Such a realization will take years to confirm because it ever resides in that little secret corner of our loving relationship with God.

The vocation really takes root when the love discovered becomes more urgent and understood. The call received in faith blossoms when it coincides with a desire that we are aware of. The determination to consecrate ourselves to God in one form or another then follows.

> In growing up, children who live in a Christian atmosphere adopt, most often in an unwitting and natural way, the forms of Christian life. It is only later that they discover the interior content of these forms.... There comes a time when the child begins to reflect and ask questions; his intelligence awakens; prayer is an exercise of conversing with God.... Still, it may happen that the child, at school or elsewhere, will hear things he doesn't completely understand, whose meaning he'll learn only by conversing with his mother. It is then that he departs from the content to find access to form.[4]

The Basis of our Choices

This is something that Adrienne von Speyr calls the road-ways of choice:

> Anyone who examines in depth the question of deci-
> sion making and looks at every angle to reach the right
> decision is frightened by the number of people unable
> to make decisions. It will be noticed that people live at
> the mercy of events and leave their existence to chance.
> They give no scope to reflection, to a meeting between
> life and the living being, and thus avoid accepting life
> by a free and deliberate act. They go through life with
> utter indifference, neither separated from it, nor really
> united to it by true self-fulfillment.[5]

Often, the call takes shape when persons, stirred out of their
lethargy, see themselves confronted by events that tear them away
from their indifference. Experiences lived out day by day and
stored in memory, gradually accumulate an array of information
from which to draw upon to make a career choice. Emotions lived
through do mark an individual. A number of experiences are
required in order to make a reasonable choice, whether one ends
up a doctor, a lawyer, a jurist, a carpenter, a religious or a priest.
It is these experiences that determine one's tastes and motivations. Look at the number of doctors whose parents were doctors!
Parental accomplishments often influence the career choices of
their offspring. The process is one of imitating a parental model.
Religious persons who are a familiar sight to children are important. Otherwise, how will a child take something unknown
to be a model? Without the possibility of seeing a religious or
a priest "doing his or her thing," how can one desire to be like

them? Sometimes it is said that what counts is our "being" in the world. Some add that there ought to be no difference between religious and secular priests. That is true in certain situations, but that is not enough for fostering vocations. This "being" has to be made visible in the here and now, something brought about by significant gestures and words conveying a personal and communitarian identity. Discretion alone is not enough. One has to see the religious and their community in action.

By now we can see the importance of the Church in Christian families. Persons consecrate themselves to God by following the example of others. This is proven by the stories of numerous vocations. The parents' Christian faith influenced the desire of the children to give themselves to God, or some cause! There are other roads that bring an individual to a religious vocation, but it is certain that the religious experience lived in one's family or with one's acquaintances do lead to the making of certain choices. Imitation is not just stimulated by the father or mother. Numerous encounters with other role models also play a part at every age.

Religious experiences mixed with practical ones in life lead to a reviewing of past events and contribute to making sense of the intuited call. In this way the future finds a framework in what has been stored in memory. Bad memories make us negative toward what we have lived through. If memories are positive, we appreciate our past life experiences. There is no question: it is better to build on something positive than on something negative.

Another example which should be eloquent has to do with violence. Where does violence come from? It is engendered by violence! The more a person sees and experiences violent situations, the more apt it is that such an individual will seek to reproduce them. Victims of violence often repeat the same conduct they have seen or undergone! Unloved young people or teenagers become loveless adults. Positive or negative events influence our desires, and people make their choices based on them.

The Birth of a Desire

Our expectations express our desires, often by following the range of our aptitudes. This is due to our upbringing and past life. The call to religious life, to the priesthood belongs more to the domain of imitation than reason. It is difficult to reason with anyone about commitment pure and simple. No reasoning process is enough to make a person choose to take the vow of chastity. It is a matter of imitation; it is a love story; it is the sense we make of it that stimulates us to take such a path. It is chosen because it is liked.

> In many of our choices that are profoundly free and often are among our most important, an attraction mostly is involved, one born of expectations and natural aptitudes; so much so that to the questions: "Why did you choose such a profession; Why did you get married to such a woman; Why are you single?" the most honest answer is the one content simply to say: "That is what I liked." "I want to be a religious because that is what I like."[6]

It is only after the fact that a person can be sure of having made good choices. I entered a community of Brothers when I was 19 or 20. It did not turn out to be a good choice. I left with regret. My questioning and independent temperament back then did not fit in with the community spirit of obedience. I had joined the Brothers of Charity with the desire of taking care of the sick, but I did not have the required submissive spirit. It was only in hindsight that I was able to say that I had made a bad choice. Before the periods of postulancy and novitiate, unlike my confreres who grew up together as teenagers, I did not go through any discernment process. Belonging to a group allowed them such a time for discernment and thus my companions had a longer maturing process. Long years of shared experiences prepared them for elaborating a choice, and served as an apprenticeship for life together. Later on many of them realized that their time for thinking things over had still not been long enough, and so they quit. Did they also make a bad choice? Others, though, stayed on. Who could have predicted that? All the factors allowing for everything to be put in place are not always perceptible right away. Later on an individual can see whether their intuition was right and whether or not they were happy.

Time for Thinking Things Over

One of the difficulties lies in making a decision. Most people hesitate to make a lifelong commitment. Already back in the 1950s Adrienne von Speyr saw how some people balk when it comes to making decisions. The difficulty to commit oneself began in the post World War II period when it was easy to get a job, and material comforts became accessible to the majority. "Time for thinking things over is something just temporary that must lead to action, decision."[7]

The time for an individual to consider their life project has become prolonged. It is protracted until a deep desire for stability takes hold of their heart. This is true for every state in life: married life, religious life and even single life. There are many options for success. To think about one's future today causes insecurity, but it can also be a source of pleasure. The pleasure of not making a decision, of going from one door to another, discovering all the possibilities life has to offer, is fascinating. That should not be surprising, and above all, not alarming. This observation should make us change our outlook on our way of accompanying vocations. It is a challenge for those involved in formation and for their communities, but it is first of all a joy to walk with persons who are subjects of God's grace, a grace which transforms their interior world, and which we are invited to discover in each one of our brethren.

How to Discover the Call via Aspirations

As we have seen, we all have to go through the stage of thinking things over in order to arrive at making choices. The spiritual guide or the one accompanying the aspirants should help them discover the fundamental option of their life along with their likes and desires, without thereby conducting some sort of inquest into the pros and cons. The accompanying helper can lend a hand in the discovering of deep-seated motivations guiding the candidate's present life. It is not religious knowledge as such that determines the worth of a call. It is, rather, an individual's underlying orientation. How does a person discover this potential which sometimes is dormant deep in the applicant's heart? Maybe it has yet to blossom. We look for the setting in which this desire can be given full scope and make this individual happy in life. The search for happiness is essential for a Christian. This happiness will surely be found in the movement toward personal conversion. However, this movement of conversion can only get launched if candidates look for their aspirations in their faith. A vocation surfaces when this interior movement leads a candidate to raise good questions about the sense he or she wishes to give to their life.

The choice won't become clear until they are conscious of this deep, characteristic desire. This desire must be discovered through other attractions that are more or less obvious and conscious. Such signs can then allow the manifestation of God's will in the matter, something of which only the person called has an inkling; so, the religious accompanying him or her must let the Holy Spirit do His work.

Rare are the vocations born of some pure and simple reasoning process. There are some, but they are exceptional. What first draws a person is the beauty and attraction of things. The vocation to religious life can only be born of the quite particular pleasure of following Christ by means of the avenue of an institutional life. A religious chooses to live out his or her baptism "with Gospel radicalism." Thus, by means of each candidate's aspirations, we must uncover the kind of deep-seated desire which is leading them to the path of their liking, so as to reach their goal and help them find meaning.

The Desire To Meet God and Set Out; an Exodus Spirituality

The yearning to encounter God and set out on such a search is the first sign to look for in each aspirant. This need is often hard to detect in the first stuttering attempts to give utterance to a vocation. A person's motivations may not have yet been purified by the fire of trials. The willingness to set out is often the fundamental attitude to get a journeying process towards God underway. Ours is the joyful task of leading people who are moving to pursue their own exodus. God is calling for such a departure. A person has to want to leave in order to become a religious. The accompanying superior's role is to keep the process on track.

> The Lord said to Abraham: "Depart from your country, your family, and your father's house for the country I shall point out to you. I shall make a great nation of you and bless you."[8]

A candidate for the religious life must accept going to an unknown country. This is the source of Abraham's great dynasty; in Jewish and Christian tradition, Abraham went on to become the Father of believers. Around him was to be built the unity of humankind after the episode concerning the Tower of Babel where we witness the rift between human beings.

Religious, like Abraham, are being called to make an act of faith by leaving their homeland for another country. Such detachment is demanding; it implies limitless hope in the One calling. Leaving something behind: goods, parents, companions, the religious attaches himself to the One who will grant posterity to faith witnesses. Like Moses, they have to leave everything so as to encounter God.

It is an important inclination: "to want to leave," "to change places" in order to enter another "country," other surroundings, so as to welcome the "promise." In that new place, the individual will discover something different, the reason why he or she has been sent, the fulfillment of their call and destiny – and without all of this being immediately apparent. So, there is the factor of the unknown in anyone's departure. The candidate sets out without knowing a great deal; a risk is involved. Can the courage to dare be found in the person interested in the religious life? Are we ourselves capable of following someone along this difficult road? A taste for risk-taking is no guarantee the trip will be a success, but it does show a determination to reach harbor.

When it comes to marriage, a person leaves father, mother, and the security of the family home. He or she has to depart, leave it all behind, to find genuine love and live out the intimate relationship of a couple. Here, too, is the aspect of the unknown. The same disquiet awaits a religious. Something has to be put aside in order to find that charitable love which leads to God. For a life of communion, a loving relationship, one has to say no to certain things or persons. This is played out most of all on the emotional level. "Therefore, a man leaves his father and mother, to cling to his wife, and they become one flesh."[9] For a certain life of communion, we are required to leave what is dear to us and what could hold us back.[10]

It is a matter of preference. "If anyone comes to me without preferring me to his father, mother, children, brothers, sisters, even his own life, he cannot be my disciple. Anyone who does not take up his cross to follow me cannot be my disciple."[11]

When someone shows up asking about our way of life, it is not that he has reached the upper echelons of mystical life. The following of Christ cannot be conveyed by some sort of harmonious description to the candidate. Maybe he is still unfamiliar with the particular distinction found in religious parlance. The search may involve ambiguities. We have to give the matter time.[12] There is a divine pedagogy which is not always easy to decipher. We have to discover at what stage in their search for God the aspirants find themselves, and how this search finds expression. What signs are indicators that they are looking for God, even if not profoundly?

Do they show any curiosity with regard to the unknown, what lies beyond? Do they realize that there may be things which are hard to grasp intuitively? There is something elusive, but they want it. Perhaps it will be difficult to engage in such talk. It may be that we'll fall short when it comes to interpreting the signs rightly, but we can surely lead others to take a few steps. Sometimes it is difficult to journey with candidates because we can't wait for them to enter the novitiate. That is when shortcuts are taken, and when people get burned, by their burning speed.

Religious life is an Exodus-like experience, and we do not always know what is at stake. Candidates for religious life leave behind their family, possessions, wealth of know-how, and often their homeland for a religious community, for a new kind of involvement. Often mention is made of the difficulties some people have today when it comes to commitment. Still, God does expect a departure. In order to discover the depths of the divine plan, an individual has to set out on a journey; otherwise, there will be no encounter. The whole mystery of the religious life is situated at the meeting point between the point of departure and the almost blind commitment to the future. There is always, inevitably, a break with the past.

When the Lord announced the liberation of Israel to Moses, it was a matter of liberation in view of future service, a mission, something to which Moses felt himself to be quite unequal: "Who am I to go before Pharaoh and lead the children of Israel out of Egypt?" However, the significant sign in the mission of Moses will be the goal of the exodus itself: "Now, behold, the sign that it is I who am sending you: when you have led the people out of Egypt, you will serve God on this mountain.[13]" The reason for God's choice of Moses, thus, leads to something after the exodus. Hence, we must not treat the immediate signs of a vocation as absolute. It is only later under the Holy Spirit's influence that we will find out whether God's will has been done. Serving God entails a sort of blindness. Too often we want the vocation's unfolding to be crystal clear. That is not God's way. To think that we possess the keys to the future from our knowledge of the candidate and the stakes involved is an illusion! But some people think that in this way difficult situations which may come up later can be avoided. That is thoroughly misguided. The "later" lies in the mystery of God, and it is in His divine Providence that the fulfillment of the call from Him is slowly realized.

As we have said, it is difficult for young people to make commitments. Even marriage is a hard commitment for them. When a person loves his or her spouse, he or she has to set out with him or her. When we love God, we have to set out and take a risk. We have to go forth to meet the bridegroom, and for religious, God is the bridegroom. Without such a willingness to set out, we will never understand the mystery of the religious life. Nowadays people make a start in it at the ages of 26, 27 or 28. Before that age, they remain attached to 'daddy' or 'mommy,' 'mommy and her home cooking,' 'daddy and his bank account.' Today people get married between the ages of 25 and 35. In Bordeaux, at the time I am writing these lines, there are three student friars who are all 31 years of age. There is a fear of late vocations. Often it is said: "Late vocations won't work out!" Culture, language, different ways of thinking, look like obstacles to us, and arouse fears in the minds of those involved in formation. With God's grace and fraternal charity, adaptations can be made for the sake of vocations of every age. I myself entertained many doubts concerning my capacity to survive my exodus. However, God's mercy and that of the community can work miracles.

In recent years, despite some failures, several people "of a certain age" have persevered in the religious life. A statistical review of the number of persons aged 35 and over who have quit is periodically published. Often these statistics fail to point out the number of younger religious who also have quit.

Moses was guiding a people on the march. Aspirants are persons looking for happiness in their life's exodus experience. They would often really like to go back to their relatives, return from whence they came (to Hobab, the father-in-law of Moses). That is just how it is in today's Church. Vocations are given to an exodus people. The Church needs the type of people who have gone through all sorts of crises, just as the Jewish people did in their day. It is a long haul before the Promised Land is reached, and it requires being on the move all of the time in order to get to Canaan.

Throughout history many Jewish people have wanted to get back to their homeland! For some the urgent calling was in their very blood.

Looking back, we, too, often get the taste for starting out again. Nostalgia about the past restrains us. In the vocation to the religious life there is a little of this illusion about easily conquering a kingdom where we will find the God of our ancestor's and be happy. This kingdom lies ahead, though, not behind. Our vocation is always threatened by the prospect of turning back. We would like to find an easier path, but to become a religious means finding ways to go forward, leaving comfort and home behind, and corresponding to the call formulated by events. The Apostles understood that quickly enough after the death of Jesus. They were on the march. They had dreams, and felt drawn by many calls. Events kept stimulating them along the path of faith. Despite fear, they went on.

The angel of the Lord addressed Philip: "You will be going south," he said, "along the road going from Jerusalem to Gaza; it is deserted." Philip set out right away… The Spirit said to Philip: "Go forward, catch up to that carriage." Philip ran up to it. He met with a eunuch whom he baptized. Then Philip found himself at Azot. He went on from there announcing along the way the good tidings in every town till he got to Caesarea.[14]

Paul's vocation was like that. He was struck blind, fell off his horse, and then had to set out to meet someone who would discern his vocation with him: "Get up now. Enter the city, and somebody will tell you what to do."[15] Someone would help him to discern his vocation more clearly. He was looking for light and would find it.

In conclusion, we have seen that the call is a choice where mediators and circumstances throw light on the path to take, but this presupposes a desire for careful discernment. Is the desire there? Without a willingness to heed events, it is difficult for a vocation to be fulfilled. We have to do some soul searching, seeking out that fundamental option which, though stimulating to us is not always clear. Throughout life the Spirit of God teaches us how to discern, making use of other people to lead us to greater clarity.

Let us make good use of the period for careful reflection which leads to a courageous choice. We have to pass from a mentality of inspector or investigator to the mentality of Apostle. It is a matter of helping people to discover God's will for them. Who cares how much time it takes?

Hardship and discouragement may beset the search. It is then that we have to come to grips with our own frailty. That is when conversion begins. To come out on top in the battle, prayer and the welcome given to grace are a real aid to the person being called. At this stage, vocations are ways of overcoming evil. That is how the march to happiness unfolds.

There are many ways to live out the Gospel. What is the best way for this or that aspirant?

CHAPTER TWO

THE SIGNS ACCOMPANYING THE CHOICE OF RELIGIOUS LIFE

What is Discernment?

To discern is to go through certain relevant stages in order to judge and make a decision. The dictionary states that discernment is the act of separating, setting aside; perspicacity, keenness in making distinctions. We speak of "discerning the truth." If a person lacks discernment, it is said that he lacks good sense. Involved in discernment are circumspection and prudence.

Isn't there a kind of ambiguity in the language we use, though, which often frustrates candidates to the religious life? By discernment we are led to understand the act of discovering a vocation and we emphasize the obstacles and difficulties. The purpose of such a process, it is said, is to discover God's call. We want assurance for our judgment, an authentication of the call. There is no hesitation in our claiming to want to help the candidate and to desire his well-being. We want to help him sort things out and find his way.

It often happens, more or less consciously though, that if a person really has a religious vocation he is above all searching for himself. Even though we emphasize the fact that the decision is up to the individual who has to discover his vocation, we have to admit that despite good will on our part, we are often out to protect our own communities from undesirable candidates. Could that be why skepticism regarding newly arrived vocations takes on an aspect more like that of an inquisition than that of pastoral accompaniment?

Who is to Discern?

Determining whether the candidate has the desired aptitudes or not is a necessary element in the discernment process, but preparing the candidate for the religious life has to be our first concern. Too often our way of doing things is ambiguous. On the one hand, we hope that the candidate will discover his vocation; as a matter of fact, though, more often than not, we seek protective measures against candidates who may spell trouble. We want to avoid failure and thus we seek security in the event of departures. We take departures quite badly as though they spell failure despite such reassuring talk as "formation is a time for discernment, for trying things out." We don't try hard enough to figure out what has happened.

Why has another person left us? Sometimes we even go looking for scapegoats. Someone has to be responsible for the situation: the candidate himself didn't know how to discern his vocation; those in charge of formation weren't up to the task or didn't see things clearly; the community fell short, or the formation system itself is defective. Someone will bring up the candidate's difficult family situation in the past. A little humility might bring us to search less for the system's defects or the candidate's mistakes, and to listen more to what life itself tells us.

The first person responsible for discernment is the candidate himself. Signs are no guarantee of his success. Discovering that he may have a vocation is not tantamount to saying that he shall see it through successfully. Recognizing certain signs incites the aspirant to align his human and spiritual tendencies aright. Inasmuch as he is the central actor in the discernment process, he has to find his proper place. In recent years there have been interesting experiences concerning modes of discernment. I am thinking of the discernment method used by the Jesuits; old as it may be, does it not remain an effective mode of discernment? France's "Gospel School" is more refined with its protracted preparatory process, where it is viewed as a place of solid preparation for vocations to the priestly, religious, consecrated or lay life. Such methods are certainly very useful means. It all boils down to the quality of pastoral accompaniment. God's call is addressed to some*one*. The invitation to think it over has to be extended, without trying to decide for the individual, without trying to protect the institution from doubtful candidates, or, what is worse, without seeking to attract only the best candidates. If God is calling, it is with the assistance of the Holy Spirit that everyone must work.

Choosing on the Basis of Desires and Motivations

What should we look for in determining the call? In moral theology, we speak of a "fundamental option." The desire to be a religious is something rather vague. Why does a person have an attraction to such a state of life? By scrutinizing desires, we enter into a world where everything may be in disarray, but where the future is at stake. It is on the basis of dreams and ideals that we forge our will to invest in the future. We must search within ourselves to discover the true, sometimes unwitting, motivations that allow us to stick things out to the end in a not always easy day-to-day reality. As we make progress in such self-discovery, we will eventually be able to make a judicious choice. The Holy Spirit does his work! "To discover our vocation means to find out what we are meant to become."[16]

The Desire to Encounter God
A God Who Makes Sense of My Life

What elements indicate that the candidate has a real desire for God? We should look for a thirst for the transcendent, a quest for the ineffable, something not easy to discern but which is there, elusive, but ardently desired. These are without a doubt some of the early signs pointing to a vocation.

The religious vocation is prophetic, bearing witness to the world of a happy life full of meaning.

> Indeed, I believe religious life is meant to be prophetic, but not as a solution to some kind of identity crises! I prefer another approach, namely, taking into account Western society's search for meaning. I think religious life is more important than it may have been in the past because of the way we are called to deal with the crises our contemporaries are going through in their search for meaning. Our life should be an answer to the question: What sense does human life make today? Perhaps this has always been the essential witness of religious life.[17]

It is in our interest to welcome people trying to give meaning to their lives, because therein, for the most part, lies the attraction of the religious state; religious should provide an answer to modern man's quest. What is it we have to offer? A great deal of patience and understanding is required of us as religious. Moreover, none of us as religious should think that we have already reached the goal. We have to be willing to run alongside someone who is slower, someone who is just a beginner.

> Though I am indeed a free man, as everyone knows, I've made myself a slave to all in order to win over as many as possible. I became a Jew for the sake of the Jews in order to win the Jews over; for those under the Law I acted as if I were subject to the Law – although I am not subject to the Law – in order to win over those who are under the Law; for those outside the Law I became like one outside the Law in order to win over those outside the Law, although rather than being outside God's law I'm subject to the law of Christ. For those who are weak I became weak in order to win over the weak. I've become all things to all men so that by every possible means I might win some of them over. I do all this for the sake of the good news so that I will have my share in it.[18]

Are we ready to become everything for everyone? To slow down our pace to take along in our trail those who run more slowly? Paul goes on to invite us to run like athletes anxious to reach the finishing line: *"Everyone who competes in an athletic contest trains rigorously, but whereas* they *do it to win a perishable crown,* we're *competing for an imperishable crown. So I don't run as if I didn't know where the finish line is; when I box, I don't just punch wildly. On the contrary, I discipline myself and bring my body under control, because I don't want to preach to others and then find* myself *disqualified.*"[19]

In our communities, we ought to find brethren on a mission. Christ is at work in them, and that is evident, because God does give Himself. We should be able to sense his presence in their daily activities. The enthusiasm involved in their quest encourages the newcomer towards new heights. He will experience this encounter with Christ for himself. He has left everything for a new world, that of the community, the commitment, the mission, the unknown.

We often hear it said that young people have difficulty making a commitment. Commitment requires detachment. There is a grace of "blindness" which makes fear vanish. Anyone who wants to get married also has to part with parents and leave their previous environment. To commit to a relationship involves risk, but love overcomes fear. A couple creates its own setting as it builds a new life, even though it doesn't know what the future holds in store. Because of their love they want to have a family and see their dreams fulfilled. It is the impetus towards the future which gives the couple its sense of commitment. The search for God, the mission, the community's charisma, the community's life and prayer provide such a sense of commitment to a religious. It is in these constitutive elements that religious life has its appeal.

A religious makes a commitment to no exclusive emotional bond except to the love of God and neighbor. He has to part with his routine and enter upon a universe where he will no longer be in control of the events, the environment, the choice of which people he will live with and of what work he will do. There will always be fellow brothers leaving the community either by choice, or on account of death. There will always be newcomers brought in by vocation or assignment. Some will just be passing through. A person has to get used to them, to adjust to them, and that won't always fall into place at the best time. Even monastic stability is not immune to change. The religious is a person on the move, headed for a not always certain future. Faith is his only certainty. Young people and teenagers come from a new culture often unfamiliar to older generations.[20]

From the search for meaning certain questions will inevitably emerge from the gradual discovery of what motivates an individual's choice. We have already remarked: a serious sign that there is a call is the desire to leave all behind, to change location so as to find another "land," another environment, in order to seize upon the "promise." Such hope lends legitimacy to departing. The individual searches for that interior space where he hopes to find that "something" different, where he and his destiny will be fulfilled through his being sent forth, and he will find true happiness.

There is a fear of late vocations. If individuals are really in search of meaning and want to give themselves to God, there is no room for fear. They will make the necessary effort to reach the goal and fulfill their dreams, sometimes at the cost of huge sacrifices, provided we give them a chance. There is no age-limit for welcoming grace. At every age people strive to give orientation to their life. That is something unique to our times. Trust is called for.

The Desire to Live in a Group

Somebody once asked me this question: "What are the values in today's world that might help the religious life to grow and expand?" One such value is brotherly love. Young people want brotherhood. They are fascinated by it, touched by it. If your community is one whose members don't speak to each other, young people won't want to live in it. To live in a group implies adaptation on their part; it is not something they are used to. Today the desire for community life is often undermined by the family or social milieu young people come from. For the group to exercise an attraction, it must live up to what it wishes to convey.

> Living in community is one of the ways of trying to answer this question in religious life. To find one's identity in community, in this friar or that sister, means living out another image of myself, another way of being human. It is the embodiment of a history that runs counter to modern hero lore. At the outset, the Dominican community used to be called a "*sacra praedicatio,*" a "holy preaching." Living together as brothers "with one heart and one spirit" was a kind of preaching, even before the utterance of a single word. Probably youngsters are drawn to the religious life more by a quest for community than by anything else. According to the Post-Synodal Apostolic Exhortation concerning religious life, we are a sign of communion for the entire Church, witnessing to the life of the Trinity.[21]

I often hear religious saying: "What counts is the desire to be missionaries, to be apostles; such a desire must motivate those who want to enter religious life." From the point of view of the apostolic ideal Jesus undoubtedly proposes, the desire to be an apostle is a very good sign of a vocation. But, for people of our day and age, this desire may easily be fulfilled in other types of life. We are living in a time when society and the Church are offering a whole host of ways of fulfilling a personal mission in the service of others without having to become a religious. So, as Timothy Radcliffe stated, there is something else motivating a person to follow Christ. There is the community. An individual seeks to live out with others a situation of Christian solidarity, in and with Christ. The community extends an invitation to apostolic action. Mission is no longer a merely personal act. It is Christ's work shared by people supporting one another, dedicating their entire lives to a particular charisma assumed with others.

Young people are very individualistic, no different from their elders, but they have an intuitive bad feeling about being alone. Therefore they need others. That is why we see bands of youths associating for all sorts of reasons, often in unruly ways it is true. Banding together gives them a sense of belonging.

I think the word "emotional" is a trap. There is a suspicion that today everyone has problems of an emotional nature. Young people have grown up alone or in small families; therefore the family is no longer that important initial training ground for relationships.

In our family there were two boys. Boarding school trained us for community living. Few people in the younger generations have had such an experience. Too often we forget that affective life is a phenomenon involving development. Stages in life are not similar. Frequently, the problem does not have to do so much with affectivity as with adjustment to new surroundings and learning how to deal with others. Of course, certain aspects of a candidate's past experience may present problems for group living. In that case we have to prepare the person, by precise and appropriate means, to live in community without too many difficulties. A former Master of the Dominican Order, Brother Damien Byrne, in his canonical visitations suggested that an effective way of preparing for the novitiate was to place youngsters in a small community with two or three friars teaching them how to live in a group. Only then would the novitiate begin. Do we put enough into this pre-novitiate stage?

The desire to live in a group is a value. As a student social worker, I was able to observe at close quarters the need youngster's have for fraternity. The Church should meet this expectation of theirs. Will it be able to regroup them and set them on meaning-ful paths? There is in France a traditional way of helping young people find their way back to the Church: walking, journeying with them and even going on a pilgrimage together. The Church in France has something to offer the world in this "pilgrimage" or "journeying" spirituality.

The desire to live with others is no indication that a person has what it takes for doing so. Besides childhood friendships (which are more or less enduring), it is school life which sets the tone for socialization. A small sized family does not always pro-vide the opportunity to learn how to live elbow to elbow, day in and day out. Parental absence means the child won't necessarily spend quality time with others. School (just as much as the fam-ily) fosters the child's social skills. School is a place for sometimes ambiguous discoveries. A child does not always know that the precariousness of school friendships risks disappointing his need to belong to a social group, but it does give him a sense of security to be part of a group that forms his identity. If in his past years group or family life was missing, he would have to find in com-munity the place to meet his need for belonging and for identity. The community will need to provide the means to satisfy such a need. It will involve steps forward and backward. Difficulties won't fail to make themselves felt. Slowly the individual will be able to develop his sense of community and his desire to live with others in a positive manner.

The aspiration to fraternity is often thwarted due to lack of a high quality social milieu. It is then that individualism risks setting in, despite other values the youth may have acquired in adolescence. A person who has developed and grown up on his own all his life is not immediately suited to group living. Here again, time matters! The quality of community life requires time for a taste for fraternal life to take hold. For some with individualistic tendencies, this development may take place later in that person's life. An aptitude for living together involves adaptation and experience.

> It could be said that in religious life we live the mirror image of the modern ego crisis. Today's individual aspires to autonomy, freedom, detachment, all of which are untenable, because one can't be fully human on one's own. In order to be fully human we need to belong to communities, whatever else we may suppose. And we as religious reflect this drama in our lives. We enter religious life aspiring to community, really wanting to be one another's brother and/or sister, but still we are products of modernity, marked by its individualism, its dread of commitment, its yearning for independence. Most of us were born in families with two or less children and find it hard to be in a crowd. Thus, today's individual and religious are two aspects of one and the same tension. The modern individual dreams of an impossible autonomy, and we religious seek a type of community we find hard to accept.[22]

Therefore we will seek to discover a person's motivations more than his ability to live in community. Next, it is up to us to foster the aptitudes necessary for community life. We will still have to allow for a long journeying process and, most of all, for an environment favoring adaptation. Here is where novitiate can prove to be a difficult time for experimentation. We should not try to do everything in the domain of the novitiate. A preparatory postulancy and a post-novitiate are required for the needed apprenticeships. That does not mean envisioning the same itinerary for everyone. In this sphere we often lack creativity and too often try to make everybody march to the same drummer. Small communities are rarely suited to preparing aspirants for common life. Communities ought to be made up of a vital minimum number of members to prevent relationships from being too strained. Likewise, we have to be on the lookout lest frequent absences bring about a feeling of solitude for people in formation.

The Desire for a Change in Life, Conversion

Wanting to live in another way should be an important sign for somebody who feels called to the religious life. One has to want to convert. Changing your lifestyle must not be an escape but a way of fulfilling yourself. A difficulty in making the choice lies in the sentimental attraction people have when it comes to the religious life, but which is not always matched by the reality of such a life. A taste for symbolism, an attraction for some type of life or other, can prompt an individual to come, see and experience the religious life. Nevertheless, the purest motivation is that of conversion to the Gospel. For some, that will mean the desire for a missionary or apostolic commitment; for others, a concern to work to advance justice; others will want to dedicate themselves to the poor. In any case, the mere desire for action won't be enough to justify a vocation. The person has to want to change his life and convert to the Gospel. Mission will be one means among others to attain such a deep conversion.

Today formation tends to be highly centered on mission. For monastic life things are simpler and clearer; when a candidate turns up at a monastery, he already desires a change in life. The concern of the director of formation is to enable that desire for conversion to emerge. Does the desire to pursue a career outweigh the desire for a change in life? It can be a bit surprising when we see a brother go back to what he left behind. Perhaps somewhere along the way the underlying desire for personal conversion lost its edge. The ardor of those early moments often is transformed into a return to the status quo. The effort to change can be trying, and only grace leads to perseverance. The stability of a religious is always put to the test by the temptation to return to freedom, to individualism, to private judgment, doing one's own thing. A confrere used to tell us: "It is not so much the reasons motivating our entrance that count, but rather the ones motivating our perseverance." One of the roles of the one in charge is to teach to those entrusted to him or her constancy and the courage of perseverance.

Given the lifestyle of people today it seems appropriate to speak about the "quality of life." Ecology is a value in our age! Young people can be made sensitive to problems of nutrition, the sharing of goods, housekeeping, heating, etc. I often say to brothers in formation: "Poverty does not mean filthiness!" There are some religious communities whose lifestyle does not offer sought after beauty. The religious habit does not always inspire admiration and respect! And there is more than that! There is "ecology" of intelligence and thinking, "ecology" in one's work, in one's motivations, in one's way of acting, which have become important nowadays. The religious life must uplift a person and inspire him to overcome sin, misery, and frailty, elevating him in such a way as to evade a certain mediocrity.

Does the candidate have the desire to live a new life in Christ? Does the community provide him or her with a chance for doing so? Are there any factors in a person's past indicating development in faith and social conduct? We are not speaking here about moral conduct as such. What we are talking about is a conversion of heart in the biblical and gospel sense. Does the individual want to live in a state other than that of ease? Will he find his happiness in the Beatitudes? God's call involves aspiring to irreproachable conduct in the Lord's sight, while at the same time ever recognizing one's own limitations. The Gospel proposes that we change our lives by imitating Christ. At this point, a meditation on the Beatitudes could well lead an individual to seriously think about the pertinence of the Gospel to his life. As religious life is a permanent state of conversion, the call involves wanting this change for oneself, not just for others. We are not dealing with some ideological level or some intellectual position about faith. We are dealing with the level of the heart, an interior inkling that "something isn't quite right." We come to realize that this "something" could be changed for the better in a different context: the religious life.

Does the person want to leave his or her old habits behind in order to choose more coherent ones in the fraternal, spiritual and human scheme of things? Or is he or she running away from a reality that they cannot quite figure out? Meditating on the Scriptures, and the Gospel most of all, is an excellent way to make a new start, a commitment to Gospel conversion. "Blessed are the meek!" but also: "Blessed are those who do themselves violence and bestir themselves to advance the cause of justice!" It is not a case of "Blessed are they who do nothing." It is not enough to be pious and kind. An individual has to take a stand for justice and accept the consequences!

In Canada there was an Amerindian uprising around the confines of a reservation close to a Cistercian monastery, at which time the monks went out to give them something to eat. They emptied out their fridges in order to feed the hungry before going to chant their Office. They never once uttered the word "justice," nor did they take sides. They were simply stating that they could not go to Choir to pray while the Amerindians had nothing to eat. That is where contemplation leads! And what about the monks of Tibhirine in Algeria? They gave their lives! That is where all their preaching ended. They died without saying much of anything at all. They survive to this day, however, as preachers for all who read their testimony.

Can an individual ever enter into a critical discussion about himself, others and the world at large? Yet that is the way a person works at his own conversion. Is she capable of submitting to the judgment of others and letting them call her actions into question? If a person lacks this critical sense, she will never be able to bring about the desired conversion. To ask for pardon implies having made an evaluation of one's actions and one's way of seeing things. The sentiment to be developed all the time is one that prods to improvement.

A religious accepts taking the last place with regard to self and all situations without blaming anyone falsely. He keeps a critical eye on himself as he marches in the spirit of the Gospel. Will he be able to rise above himself in dealing with Brother So-and-so, even if his sensitivity gets hurt? Without forgiveness, community life becomes unbearable. Ongoing rancor makes life impossible. We have to rise above sensitivity.

Pope John Paul II in his document on consecrated life speaks of our vows as "a provocation to the world." Our life calls into question those false values that make people so unhappy. Our conduct can and must judge the world. By means of our mercy and understanding let us try to stimulate a penchant for changing how things are. To do that we need to be critical in a way that is just as merciful as it is positive. We have to cultivate a manner of being that really says something to those who look at us. The aspirant to the religious life is to undertake this journey of conversion of heart.

The Desire to Follow Jesus

One has to put on Christ. There may be a vague desire to seek God, but the desire to follow Christ is not always exactly explicit. Today's adult is less conversant with religious parlance than in times past. Nor do new arrivals all have the same level of acquaintance with religious culture. Our own experience was gained over many years. We have to take into account what aspirants are going through. Among them may be some converts. Are we ready to help them out? Do they have to go through an initial period of catechesis? Learning, at any rate, is indispensable. We must help them discover in ever greater depth the Christ who will become their "Spouse."

Young people need heroes. Could Jesus be their hero? They show an interest in athletes, leaders, movie actors, and successful people in business. Do you have a hero to offer them? How about you? Who is your hero? Are you able to say so to others? When a person comes to your community, what is the first thing he sees, an institution, or people who believe in their hero? Is Jesus the sought after model? Let them spend some time with Him; then they will be able to talk about the Bridegroom, Christ. There are very lovely things to say about spiritual betrothal and the quest for the Spouse. I had an aunt who was a religious and loved to talk about her Bridegroom. She used to say she had left her fiancé for someone better. Her fiancé had come down with tuberculosis. So, my grandfather put an end to the marriage plans. She decided to become a religious. One day I asked her the question: "Come on, don't you miss your boyfriend?" She replied: "I still love him, but I have never regretted leaving him, because I've found someone still better; it's Jesus I'm in love with now." This woman had found her hero. She lived and died happily, ever in pursuit of her hero. Her smile was a reflection of her interior gladness and the joy she found in being a religious.

Trust in the Future

Death isn't something normal. Do we really want to live after death? If there is no life after death, I can see no point in being a Dominican. It would mean having sacrificed my entire life and career! Certitude is a sign of a vocation. "I have come to give you life, life everlasting." Anyone without such ultimate hope for something better will not be able to persevere amidst the hardships of the religious life. A hope, a vision for the future, is required. The willingness to live is a sign of a vocation: Christianity is not a religion of death. It is a religion of life.

I once knew a very popular Dominican nun named Sister Francis Xavier. On the day of her funeral, the Cathedral in Valleyfield was packed! The day before she died when I visited her in her hospital room, there arrived a nun from her community who said to her: "Sister, you'll soon be going to heaven." She replied in a confident tone: "Yes, but there is no hurry!"[23] She was right. To the very end a religious wants to live out God's will on this earth. We have been called to life and to life after death, but there is nothing rushing us to our death. "Give time to time," as people so often say nowadays. For the moment, it is conversion time. Tomorrow, the time for our full blossoming in the Glory of God, will come in due order.

One of my superiors used to say: "Our elders have to accept dying. They have to be realistic." I certainly do not share this view. Our community seniors have a right to hope. Can a person learn how to die? Must one accept dying? I personally don't think so. One has to want to live, do everything to live. Being resigned to death shows a lack of faith in the One Who has promised us life. Hoping to live is a path to holiness. People are praised for their serenity just before dying. Dying well is a grace they receive, accepting the inevitable, but that was not the purpose of their life. Let us, indeed, pray for the grace of a happy death, but let us not desire death. A person entering a community must be in love with life. He must desire to live with the One Who has given His life for His friends. He ought to desire the One Who make Himself present in our midst when we are gathered in His name. We should desire His Body and Blood which nourish hope all the while affirming eternal life.

Trust in the future is necessary. We must desire life for ourselves and for others. Our whole life as religious is oriented to Life. This is the promise Christ made to those who want to follow Him.[24] Young people are edified when they see in us elders the wisdom to love life.

Renunciation

The capacity for renunciation is another sign that there is a call. For previous generations vocations came through Christian upbringing, models they admired or wanted to imitate. Today vocations often arise out of suffering, a void in meaningfulness. Those who come knocking at our door will oftentimes be persons who have suffered and are in search of healing. Suffering can often be a catalyst whereby such souls acquire the taste of being loved by God and by others. In our communities do we know how to make them feel welcome? Of course, wounds may prove difficult to heal, but are our communities capable of becoming places of healing? To do so requires a certain degree of renunciation: a person accepts dying to self for the sake of greater happiness. Suffering is the sculptor's knife which carves away at us so that the beauty of his work can take shape.

The artist, the runner, the athlete, is ready to make all kinds of sacrifices in order to win, to reach their goal. A genuine desire to deny self in order to succeed indicates a pre-disposition for the religious life, which often comes as a call via intermediaries. Thus it is a good thing to trace the steps of the person seeking God in the religious life. Is the candidate conscious of the need to make a long-term commitment involving serious sacrifices to reach the goal? Individuals sacrifice a great deal for their career. Is this candidate ready to sacrifice everything for Christ, to give his life for the crucified of this world? Human destiny is beset by countless psychological, physical, material and spiritual sufferings. Would the prospective candidate be willing as a religious to assist by journeying with those who are afflicted? If he is ready to dedicate his life to the service of others, that is a clear sign of a vocation; for, like Jesus, a religious wants to give his life for his friends. He wants to live out the way of the cross in order to take along with him all who seek salvation.

The Taste for Knowing and Learning

The thirst for knowledge and for new experiences in order to move ahead and advance in life, are other signs which may indicate a real vocation. The religious life is located as much on the level of being as on that of action. Even the Benedictine tradition, whose daily life is centered on prayer and work (*ora et labora*) has always preserved the custom of intellectual work. The monastic life has always been concerned with knowing and learning. That is why monks were able to initiate such a large number of steps forward in the progress of civilization, especially in Europe. A thirst for knowledge can be a sign of a vocation, assuming the opportunity is granted. Religious communities are not associations of tailors and golfers. It is a question of going a bit further than making wafers and biscuits, honey or cheese. A religious may have to make a living by manual labor – competent at that – but, beyond that, he must never stop deepening his knowledge, particularly in the domain of faith – and take an interest in everything: from cheese to literature, from science to theology. We have to become proficient in our respective fields, while widening our knowledge so as to respond to the world's burning questions. That does not mean that all religious must be intellectuals. Nowadays one of the dramas playing out in the religious life is the failure to stimulate vocations among poor and simple folk. It is a very serious problem because such people are most appropriate for the evangelization of their peers. Furthermore, they bring realism to our communities and vigorously teach us the virtue of humility.

Religious life can answer the need people have for dignity in the twenty-first century, and on several levels. Women's role can no longer be conceived as it was formerly. The Church's credibility is at stake when it comes to the way it treats women! They are calling past practices of the Church into question. Women must remain women, with the worth of their condition ever enhanced. Monastic Orders have a role to play in the Church, as far as the plan for the advancement of women is concerned. Cultural and competent women abound; some are good at research, others can dedicate themselves to the Church by all sorts of intellectual work. Men, and particularly clerics, would do well to change their outlook on women's place in the Church, and women in the religious life must likewise update their self-image.

We must never forget that women have given creation its true focus. Mary was the mother of the Savior. Not only did she bear within herself the Son of God, she also bore an inner strength that enabled her to go all the way to Calvary and the Cross, encouraging her Son in His death.

Generosity

Generosity is an essential ingredient in the vocation to the religious life. It is among the most important signs of a vocation. And I am not talking here about obedience. Genuine obedience is generosity of heart. An inclination to generosity fills the emotional void brought about by the vow of chastity. Were candidates previously involved in social, pastoral and spiritual activity? Missionary commitment is often a sign of the seriousness of a vocation. Nowadays vocations to the religious life come from charismatic spheres where evangelizing action plays a major role.

When I asked to become a Dominican, the then Provincial told me: "We're taking a risk with you. Usually we don't take people your age (46). How things turn out will determine whether or not we take on others like you." Some years later, I asked him what made him decide to take the risk. He admitted to me: "It was because you were very active in your Church and parish. I told myself that if you were able as a layman to get involved, you'd do more as a Dominican." Capacities for commitment, a taste for missionary work, for giving of oneself, for generosity, are all signs of a vocation.

The Quest for an Institutional Form of Life

For too long we have heard this sort of talk: "Be careful not to accept candidates seeking their own security!" You would be surprised how many who said that were already secure themselves. When have we ever seen a religious lacking anything necessary? Rare are the communities out of money. Were we ever unemployed? Were we ever in a materially precarious situation that made us wonder where we would be tomorrow? The need and search for security are proper to humankind. A big heart and humility count. We entertain no illusions about our capacities. True humility of heart consists in being open to God and His Providence, and in spending time and effort to attain to something fine and beautiful. It means being realistic.

Let us find out whether institutional life can make the need for material security develop into a desire to give one's life for Jesus

Christ! Could it lead an individual to love God and neighbor? Religious living is an institutional form of life. As we all know, many active religious rejected it in the 1960s and 1970s. They did not accept it as a support. The institution must always be a means, not the end pursued. If those in charge of formation insist on details having to do with observance or the progress of the institution, it is no longer the institutional form at the person's service, but the person at the service of the institution. If we can manage to make it understood that it is the latter, with its rules, observances and way of doing things that can contribute to making a person's life happy, and if the person has such a desire, the institution can become a positive element in the formation of the religious personality and that of the community.

Many communities have abandoned the older forms of institutional life. By favoring small, more intimate communities to ensure better blending into the world, have we given enough thought to the danger of being absorbed by its way of life? Without ruling out such little communities which convey a lofty ideal of spiritual ferment to society (and its poorest members), shouldn't we recognize that for some people adaptation in such a small group has proved difficult? What is needed, it seems to me, is a long journeying process in larger groups and under more favorable conditions before reaching that capacity for living in small, intimate, groups, where proximity can grate upon sensibilities. A certain "vital space" is required for the early years of formation. Some temperaments will never be able to deal with living in small groups; does that mean they have no vocation to the religious life? Is there no scope for options that take temperaments into consideration?

Conclusion

I have outlined the desire for the apostolic way of life. Apart from the monastic life, it is something obvious for all religious life; here again, there is such a thing as monastic mission. The idea of mission or apostolate ought to motivate every Christian who wants to consecrate his life to God. Saint Thérèse of Lisieux, for example, grasped the missionary aspect of her vocation; the cloister proved no obstacle to her. Indeed, she promised that after her death a shower of roses would rain down upon the earth. Her writings constitute her mission now. She has been declared a Doctor of the Church, without having taken a single course in theology. It is possible in every state in life to be a missionary.

The apostolate is not characteristic of the call to the religious life. A person may very easily be called to become a member of an apostolic society without community living, as happens with married people who have careers in Church service (pastoral work, religious education, diocesan administration etc.). People in religious life are no longer indispensable for the functioning of the Church, or for educational and charitable enterprises. Mission is essential in all apostolic life and for all Christians, but it is not the determining factor for the religious state.

God's call is discovered by means of the signs of His presence. The invitations of the Spirit come from life. The desire for religious life has to be verified in order to arrive at a clear discernment. Let us be careful not to project our convictions as persons in charge of formation onto those presenting themselves at the doors of our communities. It is not we who are entering the community. We are already here. It is the aspirant who feels that he or she is being called by the Lord. Let us allow the Holy Spirit to do His work. As for us, let us be content to collaborate with the Spirit's dynamism.

CHAPTER THREE

WHO ARE THE YOUNG TODAY?

A First Statement

To even ask the question: "Who are the young today?" is to admit that we do not really know them. But why don't we?

We are in a "universe other than theirs." We have been living in community for many years. It doesn't matter whether we are contemplative or apostolic; some of us have broken our ties with the young. Some hearts are closed, others open. Those with closed hearts will never be able to understand the young; an insuperable distance remains between them. To understand young people we have to esteem them without judging them.

It is not out of ill will that we do not know them. Once in the world of adults, we lose contact with what a young person is living. But they are called to follow Christ just as we have been called.

A clear-sighted and adult observation, accompanied by a benevolent attitude, will enable us to enter into their mystery. We need to be shaken out of our lethargy, even disturbed! We will be put to the test, it is true. If we ask questions of them only out of curiosity, our approach will prove quite useless. We have to want to understand and enter their universe.

What does it mean to be a "young person"? The Church places them between eighteen and thirty-five years of age. Legally, they are adults at eighteen; formerly it was at twenty-one. Nevertheless, for the majority today, true maturity only arrives at around thirty. In the past, an individual entered religious life at a very young age. After twenty-five a person was already considered a belated vocation. At one time Canon law suggested that no candidate be accepted after the age of thirty-five. This stipulation was removed from Canon Law in 1984.

The Universe of the Young

Among other things, we note that young people today, for the most part, have been born into a society where certain comforts and security exist. The parents and the State protect them in many ways. Surely, there are difficult milieus. But in general, life is rather sedentary and relatively easy. Another analysis from the industrial, economical and social point of view is essential for less developed countries. In the opinion of many, vocations coming from the poor are considered suspect. Their aptitudes and their motivations are often called into question.

In the majority of cases, young people attended public schools. Religion may thus have been treated as a phenomenon apart from day-to-day life and something based more on esotericism than on reality. Religion represents something odd. Even denominational schools have difficulty maintaining the interest of the young in religious subjects. Often, the direction and the teachers are themselves apathetic, occasionally even hostile towards religious teaching and pastoral intervention in the educational curriculum. The child thus may not have a religious reference upon leaving school. Faith is reduced to a moral rule. There are no religious convictions. Religion no longer forms a part of the culture of the upcoming generation.

From their early years on, young people are exposed to the audiovisual media. The world of radio, television, videos and now the computer and the Internet, nourishes their imaginations. We can ask the following question: Is it not true that their mentality and their culture are shaped more by the media than by their family? In the universal reach of cultures, all is interchangeable, one culture influencing another. Surely, there still remain a certain number of parents determined to inculcate in their children fundamental religious concepts. They are in the minority.

Music likewise plays a very important role. It excites, and we enjoy its sounds and its rhythms. We live without any habit of silence. Until adolescence, youngsters listen passively. Then dance and physical expression emerge as manifestations of their feelings, often sexual in tone. It is easy to get trapped in a process of seduction. At the same time, drugs also are accepted as a means of escape. Almost all young people experiment with them at least once in their lifetime.

They are bathed in the hedonism that advertising places before them. All this occurs in a climate of freedom. Access to knowledge is easy for them if they want to profit from it. They very quickly adapt to their autonomy in the realm of moral decision. On the affective and material levels, because of the long duration of their studies, they remain dependent on the parents for a long time. They don't like rules and refuse to accept them if they don't perceive their coherence. They take nothing for granted. Everything is to be tried and must especially give pleasure!

It is easy for young people to travel and make discoveries.

Other cultures and countries are open to them. They can easily move from place to place. By the time of their adolescence, means of transport facilitate their journeys.

Who are their idols? I notice that sports play a very great role in their lives; since trips are easy, they benefit as much from the mountains as from the countryside. Cinema mobilizes them and influences their culture. They are energized by noise and violence, but especially by danger. Many actors are their idols. They are fascinated by the success of the stars. Imagination comes easy for them and helps them to get out of the doldrums that are so much a part of life. Video games hold their attention, especially on the Internet. There they also find an opportunity to gain information.

They seek to live in groups to fill the solitude of a limited family. The group is thus all important, because it fills the absence of parents who are often at work or elsewhere. Their friendships are often temporary.

In spite of a certain rate of unemployment, a prosperous economy offers various professional possibilities. The outlets are diverse and stir up their interest. The young invest in their future, especially according to what will provide them with security and comfort. They fear not being able to find a stable job that will provide them with material security.

They are dubbed as "dissatisfied." This is not completely true. Up to twenty-five years of age, they are generally very satisfied with their situation. It is only later that they become aware of the stakes in life and its difficulties.

They take their models from the media. Nourished by the movies and the video games, they feel the need to emulate their imaginary heroes. Their need for excitement results in their making decisions which sometimes show a lack of ethical references.

Religious models are often missing in their lives. They look for them occasionally in monasteries but also in religious sects.

Long years of study encourage them on the path to individualism; this causes a delay in the structuring of their personality. As students they learn how to work alone, without really strict and regular schedules. This gives the impression of a freedom with few limits or demands. They become accustomed to taking their time with their studies and to rushing at exam time. Regularity is imposed upon them only when their first employment appears on the horizon. They adapt but with reservation, without true commitment. Personality is structured only very late and is based on professional motivations, without personal will or sense of duty.

Values That Can Favor a Call to Religious Life

What are the positive values of the current world from which we can draw to discern a vocation to the monastic or religious life? As everyone else, vocations to the religious state seek beauty. Liturgy, music, song, arts, appreciation for nature, places away from the noise and pollution of the cities, all these are environments favoring peace. The young are accustomed to "beauty." The world presents them with many possibilities in that area during their leisure time: concerts, CDs, radio, movies (those they view being of excellent quality). Everything is available to them on the Internet. The young seek the beauty of the body. They want to remain young and they like the excitement of the moment.

Young people seek friendship and life in groups. Families today have fewer children. Crowds excite them and groups help them overcome a feeling of loneliness. A search for fraternity energizes them. It is for them a response to the anonymity of society which favors individualism.

Many are the young who aspire to do something interesting, but they reject the institution. Moreover, they shy away from commitment. They prefer networks based on similar interests where a person can enter and leave at will. They cannot tolerate the inertia they encounter in certain communities where all must obey the older members and be subject to their inquisitive eyes. This is why newer communities are gaining in popularity: there, they find they have a place. They adopt high ideals when faced with the problems of poverty, situations of injustice, politics.

At a very young age, a woman can choose to take on heavy responsibilities. Manual and intellectual work can positively affect society as a whole and the woman senses that her value is recognized. The condition of women has evolved thus allowing for a better adaptation to these new situations. Accepting that presupposes a receptive feminine community which is not nostalgically past-oriented, even if one recognizes that tradition plays a role in the formation of a person's religious identity. Often a woman is in search of her own identity and reference to the past is insufficient to provide her with a motivation to invest in a vocation or career. For example, the management of an institution, as valid as it is, cannot compensate for her desire to be a spiritual woman, capable of clear comprehension and know-how in fields up to now restricted to men. For us Dominicans, I'm referring here to preaching, to the pastoral service of the faithful, religious teaching, as well as theological or philosophical reflection. To serve the poor is not enough if they cannot have their say in the fields of social justice and the great problems challenging society.

Many young people want to give time to the marginalized, the deprived, and those excluded from the system. Others want to work in underdeveloped countries. They like being involved in associations and NGO's which address the present needs of society. Groups such as "Doctors without Borders" excite their admiration and can justify their commitment.

What Are Young People Expecting from Us?

They are better placed than I am to answer that question. But I dare to venture and share my intuitions with you. They want to be trusted by being given responsibilities, taking into consideration their capacity to assume them. Let us avoid training submissive individuals. There is often a false idea of obedience. Those in charge of forming others should not be "adoptive" or "possessive" parents of their spiritual offspring or little dictators on the spot who love to exert their power. We must be willing to take some risks, knowing that they may make mistakes and by doing so carve out their own path. The experience will mature them.

Let us easily agree to entrust our tasks to the young, giving them a place and an interest in the future of our communities. They need to make use of their creativity and to do things according to their own tastes and style. Then they will not hesitate to assume responsibility for us in hard times and during our old age.

Candidates to religious life want to be treated as adults. Let us avoid making the time of formation a time of reverting to childhood. Young people are not as young as we think they are. Under the pretext of formation, we refuse to admit that the novices and newly professed are perfectly able to assume responsibilities. Women and men who previously had responsibilities have every right to be acknowledged. Obedience doesn't mean infantilism. Spiritual paternity is not "*maternage*" or "*mothering*." Treat people like children and they will act as children. Treat them like adults, they will act as adults. The "little spiritual childhood" of Thérèse de Lisieux is related to a specific culture and to a specific time. It should not be copied, just used as an inspiration.

All young people do not think alike. It is necessary to adapt to each one of them as individuals. Did you ever ask them what their expectations were? To seek a new form of maternity or paternity with future companions or partners hampers the possibility of becoming equals.

It is often said that young people are hard to please. Are older and well-formed religious as mature as they are considered to be? Are the requirements claimed from the young in formation the same as those we ask from older ones?

The young need to feel that they are listened to and loved. They expect it. "To raise children well, one has to love them."[25] Often, we note that the elderly do not listen. They talk a lot and boast of their experiences and their knowledge. *They* know, therefore, *they* decide. How many suggestions are made by them that have nothing to do with the reality of the person in formation; indeed, frequently, their judgment comes from past experiences. A community can be formative only if it is not weighed down by its past experiences. Often our young people do not feel understood or listened to. It is an obstacle in the way of an adult formation.

Cardinal Jean-Claude Turcotte, archbishop of Montreal, said at the time of the canonization of St. Marcellin Champagnat:

> To love is not to be lenient. It is to be able to be demanding while remaining sympathetic. It is to be

able to give self-assurance. It is to believe that in any human being there is a richness which needs to be developed. To love is also to have time – much time – to listen. It is to be able to be patient. It is to be able to encourage rather than to criticize. The canonization of Marcellin Champagnat proclaims with force that today's young people, who undoubtedly need to educate themselves and undoubtedly need diplomas, need also undoubtedly to be loved. It is impossible to work at their education without loving them.[26]

In these instructions, there are two important words to help today's young people: love and listen. That means that we will not oppose our mentalities as adults to the creative and fickle passions of the young. That means that we will be willing to open ourselves to new prospects that will disrupt our pre-conceived notions and our pseudo-wisdom. Far from blocking the transmission of fundamental principles, an affectionate, understanding attitude allows us to overcome the frontiers of inexperience. Let us take a concrete example. For several years now, we have noticed an obvious need for a deeper spiritual life as young people have expressed to us. They are constantly asking us to explain the various dimensions of prayer and interiority. Unfortunately, in many religious Orders, this is often viewed with much skepticism.

Just as the birth of a child changes the life of all the family, so each generation of young people coming to us modifies our fraternal community. You come with your questions, for which we do not always have an answer; with your ideals, which reveal sometimes our insufficiencies; with your dreams that we do not necessarily share. You arrive with your friends and your families, your culture and your tribe. You come and disturb us, and this is why we need you. You generally come with requirements that are in fact essential to our Dominican life, but that we have sometimes forgotten or depreciated: a deeper community prayer life, a more beautiful, more intimate fraternity in which we care more about one another; courage to leave our old commitments and to set off on new roads. Often, the Order is renewed because young people come and insist in trying to build the Dominican life such as they read it described in the books! Go on insisting![27]

If the Master of the Order asks the young to continue insisting, it is because we have a tendency to want them to perpetuate *us* and embrace *our* views. It is as if we wanted to enlist them in our cause. Admittedly, the young need models. But they also need to create something that belongs to them and that engages them. They will look for that in the traditions that gave them an identity and that corresponded to their expectations. Let us be flexible; they expect that from us.

Their Apprehensions

John Paul II regularly returned in his homilies, speeches and letters to the question of fear in young people. Fear is a very basic human emotion. How many bad decisions are then taken because of it! It can be overcome by faith. A good catechesis to the young in formation can enable them to outgrow these apprehensions through their confidence in God.

What images of God do they have? A small book intended as a reading for young people is entitled: "The Call of God, Discernment of a Vocation." Avenger God, punitive God, remote

God, and magic God: these are some of the images of God that we must banish from our imagination if we are to open to God in confidence. I remember how we were told again and again in grade school not to "offend God," not "to make him sad." That was already better than what we likewise sometimes heard: "God will punish you." The fear of hell and of divine punishment had a preeminent place in much preaching. I do not believe that the young have been educated this way nowadays. We have evolved. The young need to hear us speaking of a God who is familiar to us, a good God, a Father God, a Mother God, a present God. Here, the Church has a role to play and has to look for this language.

> It is true that the Church must, in its wisdom and the continual assistance of the Holy Spirit, give to its faithful reference points, and preach the truth time and again, be it well or badly received. All the same however, many people see our life in God only in terms of things to do or not to do.... But, God is not there![29]

God gave the Law, but does not compel obedience. God is He who creates, gives, loves, teaches, inspires, justifies. One of the first things about teaching today's young people is that God should be for them a source of consolation. We are wounded and fragile beings but capable of great things with God's grace. Jesus came to redeem the sinner. The young person will easily understand that this God "full of tenderness and pity," who offers a hand, is the very one who wants to give him or her life and to be his or her everyday friend.

Let us give up our fear of God. Rather let us put our confidence in Him and live by His mercy and His love. Let us teach others how to maintain a concrete relationship with God. A person cannot really build a positive Christian life out of hollow speech; it is necessary to bear active witness to His presence. Our religious life will satisfy the desires of young people if they find in it a means to get rid of their anguish. Our example is more eloquent than our moralizing speeches pointing to the requirements of religion rather than to our relationship with the Lord. Those speeches are more likely to orient the religious experience toward deceptions which result in a "practical atheism." It is often the experience of sin and his own weakness that cause a man to give up faith or to put himself at the margins of the Church. Convinced that he will never be able to reach the proposed ideal, he becomes disheartened. There are many who are diverted at one time or another in their lives from religious practice and are disappointed in their experience of faith. They become aware that in spite of their fidelity to ethics and interdictions, they see themselves immersed again in their difficulties.

They forget that the mercy of God goes far beyond the image we have made of Him and His commands. Sometimes the verbal communication of the Institution veils the loving inspiration of a God who understands, loves and supports. Here, we will never meditate enough on the prodigal son "being found again." Holiness is a path. Our road is not yet at its end.

The Fear of Commitment

Very often we hear it said, and it is true, that the new generation is afraid of commitment. I dare say that this evolution has been true of all generations. In fact, however, no one fears to be happy. When seeing so many broken relations, infidelities, material insecurity, unemployment, marital violence, to commit oneself for life has become very difficult. The practice of "zapping" dominates. From a very early age, we become accustomed to choosing our TV channels without taking too much into consideration our neighbor's tastes; then, later on, we choose our academic courses already imagining the shape of our career profile; in the supermarket we choose among a multitude of offerings that feed our imagination and stimulate our craving to consume. We only rarely envision a lifetime career, except for certain professions. Young people are thus faced with the uncertainty of employment and the instability of institutions. We can therefore expect disturbances on the psychological as well as on the social level.

Where the future is ensured by a system which plans almost everything, the immediate rather than the long term is what catches the attention. Commitment is compelling due to the fact that it impedes the possibility of an about-face. Indeed, it creates moral obligations. But it is not the ethical aspect that worries the young especially. It is rather having one's hands tied by a contract for life, in marriage or in any other state of life.

We want "resolute" vocations. We want people who enter the religious life forever. We notice a great number of departures. The newer communities seem to have a better understanding of the process. To welcome, to come up with various ways of belonging, and to let the person evolve at his or her own pace in a spiritual climate, all this supports the process.

It is during this period that a person's vocation can really mature.

[...] The joy, the happiness offered to the Christian as a result of his call, is not happiness in the usual human way of thinking, nor is it founded exclusively on affectivity. Obviously, God does not deny a man natural joys such as enjoying the company of friends, of walking in nature or of being filled with wonder before a newborn baby. Perhaps, on the contrary, only the individual already capable of natural joy can appreciate spiritual joy… perhaps man at the end of this century has to relearn these simple joys.[30]

In order to determine this, we must give time a chance. Presently, I have the impression that with all the possibilities presented to our contemporaries, some essential values mature very late. It is only after realizing this that a person feels certain about his future. Up to this point, he fumbles and is seeking. This is why, today, a pre-formation is needed to discern whether or not the individual is ready to commit himself. In the same way, couples hesitate to marry; we see that very clearly at the time of their preparation for marriage.

The Fear of Rules

It is frequently said that the young seek structure and that our communities do not offer that any more. I believe that here we may be projecting the nostalgia of the past into the current situation. Fear and the desire for rules are inextricably interwoven into an ethical tendency that exists in some people. They want to find in the Church moral imperatives and reference points guiding their emotional and social lives in a sure manner. However, they are in the minority. The majority only agree to rules that motivate them. This is why they have so much trouble with perseverance. Once rules are established, they find difficulty with them. In the road leading to perpetual profession and priesthood, the will to cross the finish line keeps them going. But as soon as the vows are pronounced or the ordination is conferred, a new motivating mechanism remains to be found.

In the search for identity through symbols of belonging that link the members to one another and establish a common goal, rules can help to achieve the pursued objective. They provide structure to the personality. After the first enthusiasm, the feeling quickly emerges that the bark which protects the tree is disintegrating. What appears as a protective envelope becomes a burden and the individual seeks to escape from it. However the habit or regularity of the practices and customs remain excellent means to forge identity, to support enthusiasm, to develop a feeling of belonging, to answer the needs for beauty and uniformity leading to solidarity. They help a person to acquire a discipline which the modern world often does not tolerate. When these life habits become obligations without nuances, young people lose confidence in them and in God. Then fears and apprehensions reappear. Members become weak when structure and unanimity are no longer present to lean upon. They fail to persevere for lack of interior will. In the love of God and neighbor, however, a person *can* find the necessary support to persevere. Grace alone can guide such a process to a positive conclusion. The formative community must make itself responsible for this balance in life and support it.

Some Reference Points for Formation

In Chapter Two, we spoke at length about conversion and the desire to change one's life. Young people who approach us today asking to enter religious life or to get information about it oftentimes do so after a conversion. They don't know much about the faith and/or the life of the Church.

Here, it is necessary to distinguish between the various cultures and situations in the Church. In America situations differ from country to country. In Europe Catholic teaching is still rather strong in private schools; the parochial communities are often rather well equipped with volunteer catechists who ensure the preparation of the children. In France Christian families still provide candidates to religious life. This situation is much less frequent in Quebec, Canada.

Welcoming new converts into religious life, or others still rather inflexible on the level of their faith, can present a community with problems that are less than reassuring. That is why today much emphasis should be placed on pre-formation and a gradual entry into the community, the leadership being taken care of by personnel well trained and qualified in pastoral practice.

Personally, I found the following remarks useful; each person in charge of formation must determine, day by day, which of them is more relevant. Here, an individual's own experience plays a major role.

Speaking of the future rather than the past helps the young to integrate themselves into an adult environment. They are eager to join a future-oriented group, creating something interesting. This leads to a certain enthusiasm in relation to the life and the mission of that group. The candidate in formation does not reject references to the past if those references support a constructive argumentation. Our speech must carry a vision open to the future.

A state of life that is demanding but not fussy, inviting autonomy, supporting an assumption of responsibility, gives a certain structure to the person and reassures him.

The young need a life of beautiful, constant, regular, and

meaningful community prayer. They must also cultivate personal prayer. Places of significant silence soothe them; at the same time they need to feel the presence of others. The emulation of the behavior of their confreres supports regularity. They need to feel the interdependence between one another in prayer and observance. They are sometimes put off by the indolence of their elders. We need to teach them how to develop a certain sense of self-assurance with respect to the unfortunate bad example often encountered in the discrepancies they see between what people say and how they behave.

They also need symbols. This varies a great deal according to individuals and cultures. Familiarity and beauty are essential so that the chosen symbols take on all their significance. Newcomers like to express their spiritual progress through external gestures. Body language is important, especially for Latinos. It is not so strong among Anglo-Saxons, although, even for them, each person is different. It is necessary to tell them not to focus on observances since they are not the essential; however, retreating from them can harm their need for identity.

The new generations do not differ from ours. They refuse to accept the paralysis of institutions and require their transformation. We did the same in the past. They are also wary of those ideological tendencies which constantly try to counterbalance their possibility of changing things. Arguments from the past often frustrate the expression of their wills and so they feel put aside. Acceptance of their ideas, without prejudice, contributes to the evolution of the community. Our debates are not theirs. They know what they want and do not wish to be witnesses to our dissatisfactions. They should be left free to live their lives.

They require from us an authenticity accompanied by a certain flexibility. Their love for certain traditions and observances appears immature to us. But they must live their youth. Let us give them time to become adults; their frankness is worthy of respect.

They need a certain emotional autonomy. They do not want to be obliged to love us. They will respect us if we respect them. Realistic and true witness is essential; the style of their speech is not a provocation, but a sign of hope.

They appreciate teaching which is in line with the faith of the Church. They want honest, frank, open, joyful and positive statements. They expect a lucid analysis of society, with a vision of the future. Abusive critiques bother them. A young person said to me: "Our generation is different. We like traditional or classical liturgies but teachings that are modern and open."

The upcoming generations have a richness to be discovered and they can contribute immensely to the future of Christianity by their competence and their know-how. Let us not disappoint them.

CHAPTER FOUR

ACCOMPANYING VOCATIONS

Motivations

The motivations to enter the religious life concern two people: the candidate who asks and the guide who welcomes. At the beginning, it is necessary to be humble and realistic: Are there fears on both sides? Who wants to protect himself against whom or what? Does this very thought worry us? Do we want the good of the candidate? It is often said that "It is necessary to discern the call of God." Who are we to put words in God's mouth? On May 22nd, 1995, on the occasion of the ordination of Dominican Friars in Paris, Monsignor Claverie said: "One cannot say anything certain about God or concerning God." What wise advice on behalf of someone who was living with Muslims, endangering his life in the very name of his faith in God. The fact of living under threat in a Moslem country like Algeria perhaps makes our assertions more careful and less sure.

The persons in charge of formation are not there to decide what God wants. They are there so that the candidate can advance in the love of God and discover what he thinks God's will is. Their attitude will be more flexible. I do not say that one can admit anybody who knocks at the door. Discernment is to be exerted, which must be done in humility and truth.

The persons in charge of formation are there to guide these vocations and not to judge them. Their role is to assist the work of grace, making it possible to discern well the feelings and motivations which move the candidate. There is a compassionate, sympathetic understanding way of working with people. If certain people cannot be accepted, a refusal has to be voiced within the movement of God's love. Those in charge of formation are there to facilitate the way for someone who wants to follow Christ in a rather original and exclusive way, by discerning the signs of this call.

This is why I prefer an attitude of avoiding wounds. The person in charge of formation is there to prepare the candidate, to help him to see more clearly into himself: what he likes, what he can achieve by his own means, discovering within himself what he could do with his life. The guide does not judge in an authoritative manner. He cares about the success of the future that is entrusted to him. Time and experience will take care of a true confirmation. The one in charge of formation is to be an empathic guide; that is his or her role.

Signs have been proposed as indicators of a vocation. At a later stage, it will be a question of moving deeper into the confirmation of one's desires. If somebody would come to me and say, "As for me, I want to enter the Dominicans because I like their habit," I would be ready to accept that as positive motivation. Any motivation is to be taken seriously as well by the person in charge of formation as by the candidate. Motivations are never completely pure and limpid. If this person likes the white habit, well, if that makes him happy, so be it! God works through the complexities of our humanity. We too often tend to misjudge the motivations of others. Judgment does not always have to be made on the rational or idealistic level. God works in the heart of each one. The Holy Spirit is at work and this can be seen through events.

Young people seek to be defined as foreseeing their future in the Church. Their reflection will lead to concrete personal choices. Perhaps it will involve a penchant or dislike of the habit, or the monastery or the community, or Gregorian chant. Very few enter a community following an intellectual process. As for the question: "Why do I want to enter this community?" the task of the person in charge of formation is to lead this individual to become aware of his own answer. The purpose of discerning a vocation is not to hand the superiors an official report of the conversations between the person in charge of formation and the candidate, in order to provide them with all the elements necessary to give a guarantee of perseverance and an assurance of the vocation of the postulant. It is not that; the goal is to accompany the candidate as he enters the "mystery of his own life."

This work is thrilling. It is a pastoral work, "the pastoral work of vocations," a very beautiful ministry. What is lived with those who are in charge of formation has great value.

If they come to discern their vocation, it is a sign that, at the beginning, they have a certain confidence. That confidence has to be earned. It is not immediately given. It is necessary to allow time do its work.

Elitism in Religious Life

Monks are usually people having acquired a certain religious culture. The practices of life resulting from this religious culture separate the religious from "uninitiated persons." The members have something in common: a more advanced level of religious culture and a more developed knowledge of the faith than their lay counterparts.[31] However, in certain countries, this assertion is not completely true. There are many lay persons who have now acquired a solid religious formation.

There is a danger for monks to act like "spiritual *self-made persons*" having developed a form of elitism. A certain pride, even a certain affectation due to this knowledge can give birth to scornful attitudes. We forget that we needed years to become what we are. Moreover, we should never forget that we lived our lives in an often closed environment.

The first attitude which an individual should expect from a vocations' guide is that of a deep humility, so very difficult to acquire but so very indispensable to the exercise of compassion.

Are we intuitive enough to recognize the gifts and resources of someone else? Or are we rather bent on discovering their weaknesses which may frighten or trouble us? As human beings we are all of us always being shaped into the persons we will become. We need a whole lifetime to become the persons God wants us to be. An appreciation of others presupposes a certain modesty on our part.

For many religious, skepticism reveals an excessive amount of self-confidence. Humility has the power to make us realistic. It is one of the foundation stones of religious life. It will help us to become a little less demanding and more compassionate towards the upcoming generation. The elders defined humility as "truth," the virtue of the "just measure."

The Exercise of Compassion: Truth or Ideology

Ideologies are demonstrations of arrogant thinking. The principle of an ideology leads to a lack of flexibility: "I and I alone possess the truth!" If you want to destroy a community and its members, to cause vocations to flee, promote ideological arguments! Clergy are prone to a kind of complacency about their so-called wisdom. This is more evident in certain cultures than in others. In these cultures self-centeredness can be a little frightening. Ideology has characterized many of our religious communities during the past forty years. That comes from a kind of "intellectualism" which, according to Spinoza, is delectation in one's "thought" without putting the heart or will into it. That means that taking pleasure in ideas without regard to reality and the human person.

Thus, in religious life, members can display a great deal of idealism. But the elbow-to-elbow situation in which they live constantly reminds them of the harsh day-to-day reality. Through its setbacks, life teaches us that the road towards the ideal is very long. Only compassion can soften the rough moments of a completely dedicated life, without the hope of immediate gratification.

Elitism often leads to ideology, a negative agent in the natural evolution of a human being, leading us to make judgments without taking into account God's creative action that, by the Holy Spirit, by His inspiration and His gifts, constantly makes us grow. Very often ideology is a sign of a pretentious attitude vis-à-vis others' behavior and moves away from the truth by putting aside the need to give testimony in words and deeds. The fact of remaining on a rather ideological level, without taking into account human limits, leads to very unrealistic ways of judging, not taking into account the evolution of persons and institutions. Ideology discourages creativity.

The ideal, by itself, is noble if it is a goal proposed to be carried out by everyone. Religion is a dangerous environment in which we are always tempted to compare others using ideology as a yardstick rather than the ideal. Religion can prove to be a real danger by locating the individual in an ideological space without taking into account his psychology and essential needs.

Ideologists frighten me because they draw us into an imaginary world more fictional than real. Jesus spoke to the average man or woman on the street. While remaining one with His Father, He was incarnated. Wasn't the ultimate motivation of His life to save ordinary human beings through His works? For Him, it is a question of communion with His Father *and* with humanity. The history of Jesus and His mission supposes the experience of human life and a relationship with human beings leading to the realization of His own works. "The words I speak to you I don't speak on my own. It is the Father who abides in me who is doing His works. Believe me when I say that I am in the Father and the Father is in me. Or else believe because of the works themselves."[32] It is a question of dialectics between presence and action generated by a relationship of intimacy with His Father. Ideology distances us from this divine space, looking at us from above, locking us up in a purely idyllic fantasy.

In recent years, we have known an extremely favorable movement toward social justice. When I began my formation, it was required that everyone be interested in that movement. It was *"politically correct"* to believe in it. Even today, in certain communities, a formation course in "social justice" is mandatory. To preoccupy your self with the poor is judged to be something positive. However, religious communities have been concerned with the poor for hundreds of years. To put too much emphasis on that and to make it mandatory brings, as a consequence, diminished interest on the part of those who never worked in those areas or who do not feel capable of doing it.

One person identified himself with a very beautiful ideal. But this "ideal" then became an "ideology." You couldn't be a Dominican without being favorable to it. At the time, Albert Nolan was for us an extraordinary human being! We all would have liked to be "Albert Nolan," courageous defender of the rights of the Blacks in South Africa. But we must be what we are called to be. I was fortunate in having persons in charge of formation who understood that. It is *not* necessary, in the name of an ideology, to compel a person to become something that is not in their character. It *is* necessary to lead them to a consciousness of certain things, while respecting the personality of each one. In addition, no society is perfectly homogeneous. The world is a universe of differences. We cannot all have the same sensitivities. Tomorrow's religious will not be certified copies made in series for the Church. Each religious has to realize his or her personal charism for the common good. They will do it by turning their personal motivations and aptitudes into something profitable. The identikit of the ideal religious does not exist. The day that happens, we will have to destroy it as quickly as possible. If not, it will destroy the Spirit who is at work in each of us.

There was a time when small communities were *à-la-mode*. People did not believe in big communities any more. A whole generation looked upon big communities as breeding grounds for individualism and community indifference. Many were the campaigns to incite congregations to eliminate them.

We quickly discovered, especially in men's communities, that some people are unable to live in small groups. Several left them disillusioned by their experience. To be sure their failures hurt them. Other confreres continue to believe that this is the only way to live the Dominican life having lost faith with respect to big communities, and this has been the cause of much discord. The true question is not there. It is a matter of taste and aptitudes. Today, we are a little more realistic. Pluralism in types of community life is better accepted. But how many fights we could have avoided!

An ideology is an abstraction which does not take into account the concrete situation. It would have been necessary to say: "If you want to live in a small community, feel free to choose to do so."

Monastic communities are not immune to these problems. And women's communities have particularly been put to the test. Often, *"self-proclaimed experts"* came along with their solutions which did not always serve the common good.

Many candidates to religious life are molded by ideological systems even before they enter. They may have gone through many conflicting experiences. In working with new vocations, it is necessary to avoid speaking authoritatively or giving an opinion regarding ideologies. It is rather necessary to respond as adults capable of leading the person to leave behind such ideological systems and to bring the candidate back to what is essential. This supposes that those in charge of formation are not allowing themselves to be trapped by their own ideologies, inherent to the human condition. Some elements of religious life are essential, some are specific to the charism of the community, and others are of less importance. We must know the difference.

The persons in charge of formation must do their best to orient candidates so that they become aware that any ideological system must be submitted to two processes: first of all, a screening according to the Gospel; then a confrontation with the realities of everyday life. These are the best means to succeed in helping people progress and to get rid of those systems that deprive them of their freedom. Ideological systems imprison an individual.

Speaking at length about "ideology" is important, because ideologies violate the fundamental law of compassion. Any human being has a right to freedom of thought. The person in charge of formation has the duty to be compassionate if one of his or her candidates is mistaken and receptive if he or she is right.

The Candidate's Personal Background

The distance between the experience of the guide and the naivety of the candidate differs. Therefore, a degree of frankness is necessary if an individual wants to become a religious. Faith invites him to adopt that attitude. After 20, 30, or 40 years of religious life, certitudes and opinions are acquired. We do not have to expect that the person whom we are walking with be of the same opinion as we are. And this distance is very important. People are afraid to enter a community because of a certain image of community life that they have. Sometimes it frightens them. An "inquisition" attitude provides a more or less accurate image of religious. It is normal to find differences between generations; it is necessary to take them into account. To that end, we have to promote better communications, each one respecting what he is while leaving possible disagreements out of the picture. It is the whole question of otherness which is at stake here.

Let us avoid trying to trap people. Let us be natural and frank. We should be able to listen to others, accommodate them, and inform them without *a priori* opinions or prejudices. Our questions must be objective and unobtrusive. The guide must establish a dialogue with the candidate and move it along.

It is very important to know the personal background of the candidate in order to act with discernment. Unfortunately we often tend to act "off the cuff." To help a candidate adapt, we have to build on his background and his experiences. These are the starting points from which we will slowly be able to discover if there is a vocation.

The appropriate questions should be raised. There are many things in our lives that fall within the realm of the subconscious. One of the guide's roles is to make the candidate more aware of these. Thus the candidate will come to discover his or her vocation. The candidate should take into account the difficulties that he or she could come across in their adaptation, their relationships with others, the challenges represented by silence and other regular observances, by a form of solitude compared to the outside world. Difficulties and limits will then be better identified and evaluated.

Vital Strengths of the Individual

Through this dialogue, a person's strengths and weaknesses will be discovered. Let us not put emphasis on the weaknesses, but rather on the strengths. "When you evaluate a preacher, look initially at his qualities and build on that," a priest who had been teaching public speaking for years told us. "As for the weaknesses, in the end, you can always offer a comment, but gently."

Can the candidate make the charism of the community his own? Certain clues will work in favor of one community more than of another one. The person in charge of formation should not hesitate to stress them and to discuss them. By scrutinizing the candidate's life experiences he can discover aptitudes for this or that type of vocation. It is advisable to seek the vital strengths to build upon.

l) Is the person sufficiently dependable to engage in the charism of the community? To know that, it is necessary to examine the person's life. What tasks or responsibilities was he or she entrusted with? Did they show an interest for a certain sphere of activity? Were they in the labor market and were they able to make decisions and to manage their lives on their own? A steady employment before entering indicates a capacity for assuming responsibilities toward self, which is very desirable for the positive development of self-love and love of others. Such an individual will be able to take into account the requirements and obligations that will be proposed without dramatizing them.

2) Is the person able to live up to the challenges which are offered? Does he or she want, for instance, to take up the challenge of the Benedictine life? Are they able to do that in a responsible way, based on the successes which they have experienced before? And if we discover that they have had none, is it preferable to wait and encourage them to get some positive work experiences before entering? After entering, they will be able to better appreciate their progress. We don't build up someone's personality by emphasizing their problems and defects, but rather by emphasizing the positive aspects of their life. These are to be acknowledged and developed.

The aspects which form a candidate's identity must be emphasized. A person's identity is created taking into account how they handle conflicts, the person in charge of formation being one of those with whom they may have had some conflicts. This is perfectly normal.

3) As for emotions, does the person spend all his or her energies in personal gratification? Does he or she remain on the level of desire or fantasy, without concretizing in a coherent way what justifies this? There are people who act under the impulse of emotion. Is such a candidate able to go beyond this level and be ruled by reason? If he or she remains at the level of desire or fantasy no progress is possible. It is necessary to attain a level of personal conviction and commitment. It is at this point that the strongest desires take on significance. Passing beyond immediate gratification leads to self-mastery and lifts the individual up to the spiritual level. A positive return on past actions gives the candidate an opportunity to appreciate the results of his or her efforts and encourages him or her to progress in this way of acting; hence, the importance of seeking what is best in an individual and giving positive affirmation.

4) Is the person capable of becoming conscious of constraints and of assuming them under the supervision of someone else, in total freedom and with a sense of duty? Does he or she assume their responsibilities? The superior or the person in charge of formation can point out or ask them to do something, but not all acts of obedience become acts of virtue. The person should be led to understand the coherence of the request. He or she must grasp the importance of the need at stake; to see that such a thing is helpful! By collaborating in a community project, the candidate will feel that he or she is making a positive contribution for the advancement of everyone. Obedience is a way towards the appropriation of a sense of community and its mission. That mission exceeds personal needs or expectations. Out of that comes the pleasure of obeying. Logic is necessary in the act of obedience.

5) Is the person able to make decisions freely that could lead

to a final commitment? Are they able to commit themselves to God and others in a long-lasting way? In the case of instability, a lengthier postulancy may make it possible for them to do so.

Purity of Intentions and Commitments

Can intentions always be pure and reasonable? They often overlap and intermingle without being as coherent as we would like them to be. In the desire for religious life, it is necessary to determine the unequivocal intention to find a direction for one's life in the joy of giving oneself to Christ. The attachment to Christ and his Church is essential for such a step to be one that will likely carry on. But this intention will always be accompanied by desires and motivations that are ambiguous. When Jesus met the people of His time, He sought in them a sense of faith. We must also seek this adhesion of faith. For the rest, it is really necessary to put our confidence in the Holy Spirit. It is by adhering to Christ, by seeking God above all, and by being attentive to the inspiration of the Holy Spirit that anyone will really be able to say "yes" to the choice of religious life.

Let us remain completely humble before the mystery which is revealed in the person of the candidate. Let us learn how to discover the creative work of God which manifests itself little by little. Let us accept that each and every person is a work in progress and that today is only the beginning of God's intention for him or her. Only eternity will really reveal one's personal call.

A good preparation facilitates the future formation of the candidate. Let us not hesitate to prepare well those who are longing to follow Christ. Jesus took a long time to form His apostles.

CHAPTER FIVE

PRE-FORMATION

To Be Successful: A Gradual Entering

Pre-formation is a concern for many persons in charge of formation because it inevitably evokes the almost universal need to fill the candidates' lack of preparation. So often we find ourselves dismayed by the candidates' lack of knowledge and aptitudes. Businessmen face the same problem and complain about the fact that governments, public personalities, persons in charge of education are not preoccupied enough with an immediate and better adapted preparation for professional life. Employers must complete the training of their new employees so that they can adapt and become productive in a specialty corresponding to the needs of the company. In 1973, Canada created a formation center for the personnel of "Income Canada," a division of the Department of Taxation because it was noted that the university graduates lacked the necessary training and experience. A program had to be instituted to prepare the ministry's future managers.

Years back it was customary for a person to initially become an apprentice in a trade or a skill. Wages were lower because the company considered that it was thus making a capital investment in the person for whom it was providing this training and experience in a work environment. Today, companies only wish that the government, schools and other institutions would assume this task.

Religious face the same problem it seems to me. Why weren't these future vocations properly prepared? Why wasn't the family or society capable of helping these young people to grow towards their full maturity so that ultimately we could accept them in our communities? And what can we say about the Church and Catholic teaching?

Catholic schools played the game of competition with respect to the public system of education. To attract consumers, they easily accepted a plurality of religious options, allowing students not to register in religion classes and to choose other subjects instead. In certain Catholic schools, there is almost no pastoral involvement on behalf of the Church. The lack of collaboration on the part of administration and faculty is likewise apparent. Some are even uncomfortable choosing an educational environment labeled "Catholic" for fear of being ridiculed.

There was a time when the school imparted a more general education and the means to use it wisely. The family did its best to educate. Seminaries, pre-formation schools and juniorates, as well as colleges then took over to prepare young people for a religious, priestly or professional vocation. Women's communities accepted candidates more easily without much preliminary preparation. And for good reason! The woman was the teacher *par excellence*. She was gifted to prepare herself for Community life. She was the pillar of the family and, from her youth on, she assumed broad responsibilities in the family. She became mature at an earlier age.

Do we idealize our past too much? Let us not forget that

Catholic schools compensated to a large extent for the deficiencies in family education. Piety was part of a child's cultural environment as a Christian. This is no longer the case today. Many families are in shambles. Religious teaching is often flawed for lack of qualified or motivated catechists and the new technologies of communication put at the service of education and faith are only beginning to bear fruit. They are not yet, however, sufficient to penetrate the world of young people.

The Family Background

It is essential to keep in mind the most recent experiences and education to detect the candidate's aptitudes for religious life. These factors will determine the sort of guidance and the voids to be filled. One must arrive at this information through an open and tactful dialogue. Informative allusions can lead us to discover what the person has gone through. At this point in time we can begin to establish where the candidate may be in relation to his or her faith and religious culture.

Candidates to religious life come to us from various family environments. Some will be from stable families with many children in which the evolution of the person will have been more flexible and less disturbed by parental conflicts. These candidates are lucky and will likely follow the parental model. They will be better prepared to follow either the path to marriage or to religious life. But these candidates will be exceptions, since divorces exceed 50% of most contracted marriages in the "civilized" world today.

Should we then throw up our hands in the face of possible problems? In my opinion, this situation should question and stimulate our creative imagination, inviting those in charge of formation to a profound evangelical reflection. Religious life has to answer the call of those who want to embrace it. It must do so with courage, skill, compassion and mercy. Psychology can help in this area. Courage and tenacity will be required to adapt our methods of formation to the current sociological context. We will be blessed if evangelical convictions animate us.

Pastoral Aptitudes or Psychotherapy

The person in charge of the acceptance of candidates is not a psychotherapist. Nor does he have to become one. He must remain hospitable, in the very way Jesus received the rich young man and the apostles. The promotion of vocations is not a Church therapy service. It forms part of our mission of evangelization. It especially asks of us a great proximity with Christ in order to better allow the call to be heard. However, it is in human soil that grace operates. No one becomes a religious by way of a char-ismatic awakening in the Spirit. We become a religious in our flesh. Things do not fall immediately into place and we need to pass from an initial attraction to a surrender of the will.

> Once the call has been perceived, the will recognized, and the choice made, the candidate is generally in a state characterized by the following facts: both the will to which he subjects himself and the submission itself might well be valid; it is nevertheless the case that they do not yet coincide completely. He said "yes" to the invitation to grow into a certain vocation, and this yes is naturally the prerequisite to the growth. But while waiting, there exists nothing more than the declared

will to go where God wishes him to go. This declared
will opens the way and also allows early discernment
of some aspects of it. But it is not yet itself the actual
way.[33]

It is necessary to prepare oneself to live this call. The way to
be followed has hardly been opened. And it is here that the social
and family antecedents of each candidate reveal their importance.
It is the human soil with which it will be necessary to work.

How should the director proceed? There is no doubt that
questionnaires are available and one can easily obtain a number
of them. I do not believe that this is the ideal method. These
questionnaires should only be used as guides for the person in
charge of formation. In my opinion, we are not "inquisitors" who
scan people's past to protect the community from candidates who
could possibly cause problems. We are guides, apostles, friends
of Jesus and we seek to bring other friends to Him.

Regular visits of the candidate to the community or friendly
conversations, even by phone, are more valuable than any psychological evaluation made by an expert. Moreover, experience
shows us that very often these tests are misleading. There is no
valid test showing with certainty the sincerity of the heart and
the degree of faith. The danger is that these tests take responsibility from the person in charge of formation's shoulders. It is
easy to spontaneously transfer the decision making responsibility to a third person. However, the decision makers must be
personally involved: the person in charge of formation and the
candidate. This is admittedly difficult and sometimes unpleas-
ant, but involvement is necessary nonetheless. In certain cases
it is true a personality test may be valid for better orienting the
formation of a candidate and informing him or her regarding

certain character features which could present some difficulties. However, one would need to pay attention and respect professional confidentiality. A leak can weaken, if not break, the bond of confidence which must exist between the person in charge of formation and the candidate.

A certain period of time is needed to get acquainted with the candidate. It also helps the director to better know him and his aspirations and provides an opportunity for him to speak about his family, education, work, desires, and hopes. It is through this dialogue that the director really discovers the person. Here also, one can detect his progress, the depth of his faith, and the purity of his intentions. But who enters religious life with a completely pure intention?

Frequent visits to the community also enable fellow-brothers or sisters to detect certain aspects of the individual's personality. Without revealing purely objective criteria, their remarks can contribute to good guidance. Certain people will come to us wounded by life. Let us not reject them immediately. We were all wounded in one form or another. Jesus did not come for those who were saints but for those who were sinners. In recent years, we have tended to forget this in religious life. This is why new communities have such success. They accept that the community is a place of cure for certain people. On this topic it would be interesting to read Jean Vanier's book: *La communauté, lieu du pardon et de la fête*.[34]

Very often a pre-formation would have helped avoid departures during the novitiate or the years of temporary vows. There are certainly wounds which are slow to heal and which, because of that, are obstacles to a satisfying religious life. To solve certain problems, it would be better to delay entrance and to suggest guidance from a specialist. Once this is done, adaptation to community life will be easier. Guidance from the person in charge of formation should be handled in stages tailored to each candidate's needs. Since we tend to develop structured systems of formation according to time and place, this pre-formation must be done outside of a rigid framework. Isn't life the best way of structuring personality? Formation must envisage stages and means so that the candidate acquires certain habits. For those who might need it, schools or groups can play a role.

The perfect personality, with a mature religious and psychological profile, does not exist. Our desire to welcome only those presenting an ideal profile often prevents us from investing our energies into the preparation of these people. We want to have our cake and to eat it too, while forgetting that it was initially baked by another baker. In many traditional religious communities, the acceptance of candidates to the novitiate is too quickly agreed upon.

Thus, preliminary guidance must identify the strengths and weaknesses of the individual in order to lend the necessary assistance.

The Pre-formation Steps

The initial request

The first contacts should allow the candidate and the person in charge of formation to identify if the felt attraction is confirmed by an awakening of appropriate motivations and aptitudes. It's up to the person in charge of formation to make use of these initial contacts to carefully document the candidate's file. Currently, we can say that the quality of this documentation often leaves something to be desired. Documentation and good record keeping allow for a better knowledge of what is at stake in religious life.

Well transmitted information makes it possible for the candidate to distinguish by himself if such and such a project is appropriate for him. This first stage supports the development of a still unexplored reality. To join a community, is to join a family which has its own characteristics.

Once this information gathering stage is completed, we enter the phase of understanding acquired by contact with the candidate's acquaintances and environment. This second stage opens the door for more frequent contacts. Indeed, each community has its own modes of operation, its manner of communicating, its very personal intuitions and its way of approaching people and ideas. It can be a closed circuit. We are embarking here on a process of discovery. Surprises are often caused by hasty entrances without preparation, sometimes degenerating into emotional or untimely departures. They are painful for both sides. They leave a wound which will take the individual – also the community – a long time to heal. The person in charge of formation is there only to accompany. Jesus did not throw anybody out. It is certainly demanding work requiring a lot of patience! That may at times require a certain assertiveness. The individual who does not have the capacity to manage aggressiveness is not fit to be the one in charge of formation, nor the Superior.

Contacts with the community

From the time a prospect senses a call, the intuition of a desire, until the realization of happiness in religious life, there is more or less a long lapse of time depending on the candidate. One thing is certain: today the person wishing to become a religious must expect to gradually enter the mystery of a more or less diffi-cult life which requires human, cultural and religious adaptation. This process has to be made according to the capacity of each one to assimilate a number of changes in attitude, behavior and know-how which will lead him to his ultimate blossoming.

This preparation begins with the experience of living with the members of the community. It is necessary to develop various friendships, because, with the person in charge of formation, there will always be a kind of "father-son," "mother-daughter" relation-ship. The candidate can count on these other new relationships. When difficult events come up, the person can exchange, discuss, and ask for help to overcome personal resistance. He is entitled to be wrong or to be right. The confidant can play a very positive role by being an attentive listener. That supposes that the person in charge of formation does not feel threatened by such conversa-tions. The persons in charge of formation must rather encourage this dialogue, to solicit information about such assistance and to be delighted that the aspirant is comforted by it. While sup-porting the authority and showing understanding, the confidant contributes to the progress of the formation of the candidate. In the Dominicans, the assistant-master often played this role in a positive way by allowing the candidate to blow off steam at the time of conflict which might exist between the authority, the candidate in formation and the community.

There are moments when a person needs to cry. One should not be afraid of it. The Son of God suffered; did He not say: "*Why did you abandon me? But not my will but your will be done*"? The elders have a very important role in formation. This all starts during the time of pre-formation; there the climate of confidence develops. If it is normal to feel a certain affinity towards someone, it is also important to avoid harmful particular friendships. It is very destabilizing for the persons in charge of formation to see young people clinging tenaciously to the friendship of an elderly brother. It is necessary to take the risk and to prevent that these friendships do not become possessive, even dependent. The first contacts with the community remain a privileged moment to find models. Consequently, the role of elders is important for the perseverance of a vocation. Very often, even after their death, the elders continue to transmit to the young the message of courageous fidelity through all the vicissitudes of life. They remain a point of reference which we enjoy recalling to mind. They continue contributing by exerting a spiritual "maternity" or "paternity" and we maintain a filial devotion towards them. Their departure is a loss; their memory, a richness.

Conditions for the period of training

Monastic communities envisaged more or less long training periods for the candidates. The stages were to provide a moment of positive appreciation of community life. They were useful to discover if the person is able to subject himself to the asceticism of regularity and if he can live the possible tensions of a community life. One sometimes has the impression that communities use these training periods to protect themselves against the risks of a difficult personality.

A training period should be a time of loving contact with the life and intimacy of Christ. Apostolic communities should also envisage some similar periods. Admittedly, they will be different, but they must be strong moments where the person experiences the love of the Lord and the joy of serving Him in the apostolate. Active communities are beginning to envisage training periods in their apostolic projects where real life is found. Times of voluntary work in the service of the charism of the community allow a candidate to get acquainted with that community's way of life. These training periods can replace the formation which our seminaries used to give. Currently, there is a tendency to place them after the novitiate. In my opinion, the second year of novitiate is no longer necessary since people enter at an age where they already have a good experience of life. I rather believe that the training period, even the apostolic one, must be done before entrance, because it can help a vocation to mature. That, of course, supposes that the community will welcome the candidates with compassion and broadmindedness. Other equivalent experiments will be made to strengthen the vocation after the initial formation.

Candidates should not be privy to the controversies of the community, without however hiding difficulties. It is important that they become conscious of the positive aspects of community life. The presence of candidates in their midst provides members an occasion to improve their communications skills. They become more careful to control their language, to avoid criticism, not to focus on their pet peeves. These are all virtuous practices which ennoble religious life.

We are astonished lately by how difficult it seems to persevere in religious life. Wouldn't it be better if our communities give to each religious member a quality of spiritual and human existence which supports perseverance? Newcomers expect that. In communities, contemplative or active, the danger exists that frustrated religious "confide" in the candidates. This provides an occasion for the person in charge of formation to speak with the candidate to ascertain the candidate's judgment and his will to adhere to the group in spite of perceived "flaws." By being able to overlook many things, the candidate goes beyond the stage of infatuation with the community.

Study

We mentioned the role of former seminaries as well as pre-formation houses and juniorates. There now are schools of theology, seminars on faith, faculties of philosophy or theology, and reflection groups that can give structure to religious thinking. Study is fundamental for religious. It should not have to be at the university level. Postulancy, for example, could be a time of study and reflection with colleagues. In Canada, very often, the Dominicans required of their candidates, especially if they were very young, to make their two years of philosophy before entering the novitiate. After this experience, most of the candidates persevered in religious life following their novitiate.

Wouldn't it be possible for apostolic communities to begin their formation cycle with periods of study also? A master of formation other than the master of novices would be better situated to accompany the candidates and to prepare them for community life and the acquisition of religious knowledge. The postulancy could vary according to each one's needs. Today, there is no longer a specific age for study. We should open the door to an '*à-la-carte*' and well-adapted formation.

Regular and well-prepared interviews

The interview seems to me the most practical and most functional tool for the preparation of candidates. There, listening is fundamental. A way of proceeding is to note in writing the important aspects of the conversation to avoid interrupting; then possibly refresh the conversation by questions. Personally, I destroy the notes in front of the person, thus avoiding creating the ambiguity of a filed document. All religious have a right to their privacy. The subject in formation will not engage in confidences if he has the least doubt about the discretion of the persons in charge of formation. The interview is concluded by a synthesis underlining the strong and the weak points.

This meeting is the ideal means to bring about progress. During pre-formation as well as during the formation period itself, it must be regular and obligatory, but in no case threatening. The master needs tact and much simplicity. A paternal attitude has its place at the right time, but the master is also exerting his role here as a teacher. He is not only listening. Nor is he a therapist either. It is an adult dialogue between two people. It is necessary that the religious in formation feels that. The interview is seldom the occasion where authority is exerted. Firmness is exceptional; compassion is frequent, and prejudices are overcome.

Humility plays a paramount role. It is necessary to admit it if and when one is mistaken, to move back when faced with aggressiveness, to move forward in the presence of joys and successes, to listen in times of difficulty, and to accept defeat gracefully. Then, there will be an authentic relationship and real guidance.

Discretion

Confidence will be a result of the discretion of the person in charge of formation. The master of formation is not confessor of the brothers in the Dominicans. This is required by Canon law and our Constitutions. He is named and not elected. It is one of the rare functions whose nomination is not subject to the elective process of the brothers. One can see the importance given to this responsibility. His first role is to listen. Discretion is a centerpiece of the relationship and only by it is confidence ensured. All is not to be revealed. Thus, the master of formation will be vigilant in order to never break confidence.

CHAPTER SIX

ADAPTATION TO RELIGIOUS LIFE

A New Phase: The Formation Itself

Many subjects previously dealt with are more or less connected to the adaptation to religious life. This adaptation is not separated from the phase of discernment, just as the period of pre-formation is not without consequence on future formation. Adaptation to religious life takes place throughout the entire period of formation. The candidate adapts to religious life insofar as he progresses in his relationship with God, in personal conversion and in his openness to the other members of the community. It is a question of growth. "We will really be Dominicans at the moment of death. Up to that point, we attempt to arrive there," said my master of novices.[35] It is only afterwards that we really become conscious of the call which was directed to us by the Lord. The same applies to our progress.

Formation begins as soon as the request is received. Pre-formation and the initial formation must be lived in continuity. That supposes that the preliminary stages of consideration and discernment of the vocation were lived and assimilated. Bypassing one of these stages runs the risk of putting unquestionable vocations in danger; but little can be done to prepare an individual for the religious style of life. Religious communities have difficulty overcoming the "institutionalization" of their lives in order to arrive at the "humanization" of the institution. To humanize it, it is necessary to tend to a greater diversity of means.

Formerly, there was often confusion between the goals of the institution and the components of the religious life. The institution (the apostolate or structures of operation of the congregation) was positioned above the spiritual and human needs of the persons.[36] Needless to say, such was not always evangelical. The needs of the mission took precedence over any phase of humanization. It was necessary that the apostolate be efficient, therefore it had priority over spiritual and human needs. At the same time, there was the insistence on maintaining religious observances without prejudicing the sense of duty and responsibility at work. It was necessary to live everything intensely and at the same time. The chapter of faults and the advice of superiors emphasized one or the other of these aspects. The state of evangelical perfection became the state where all had to function perfectly, with the risk of breaking the equilibrium of the individual. Caution is to be taken to avoid dispersion and overload if religious life is to be lived by contemplative and apostolic persons. It is easy to create an over excitement, preventing the gradual adaptation of the individual to the rhythm of the life. This hinders the development of a profound interior life. Religious, like all human beings, need a peaceful and serene environment to progress on both the spiritual and community levels.

Entry into Religious Life

The test of perseverance

Those who enter a community today know very well that few religious have persevered in religious life since the Second World War. *"Many have been called but few have been chosen."* We have all known priests, religious or nuns who left. They shared their doubts and their disappointments stemming from more or less painful experiences. Perhaps there were disappointed religious among the members of their families and those may have had a positive or a negative influence on their decision. These situations have caused them to question themselves. For a few years now, the media informs them about certain scandals. Will they be able to persevere until the end in spite of appearances which seem difficult to reconcile with a desire to follow Christ? If not, what will they do if the time comes when they feel they may have to return to the labor market?

Moreover, conversations with elders about such and such individuals who left the religious life will not fail to stir up their curiosity, their concerns and sometimes their anguishes. Am I like those who gave up? Have I adopted the same attitudes, the same defects? Will I have the same difficulties? What will my future be in the Congregation or Order? In the long run, will I be accepted with all my limits, my concerns, my temperament, and my manners of acting and of thinking? Vis-à-vis the vows and the temptations of the world, will I be able to keep on going?

They also have the example of many couples who did not persevere in their marriages. All these difficulties, of which they are well aware, throw doubt on the possibility of persevering in almost any state of life. They live in a society where it is easy to switch from one professional vocation to another. On the other hand, we invite them to remain faithful to the end, for their whole life. Little wonder it provokes their concerns.

The apprehension of a new culture and a structured life

Contemporary life is a life of freedom where, outside the professional framework, everyone thinks of himself or his family. He who becomes a religious may have considered marriage. Perhaps he experienced a close relationship with someone. He managed his life and his emotions freely, in his own way. Henceforth, he will have a framework imposed on him, sometimes a rigid one. His whole system will have to adapt to that. In community life living in relative seclusion will be a disconcerting experience. At the time of a first meeting, he will have been provided with a certain amount of information. Now, he will have to live up to that. This loss of freedom can lead to a certain sadness and dissatisfaction. No more deciding your own agenda, your own leisure time, your own place of work, your own activities; these are just some of the limits that the person discovers day after day.

This freedom will be seriously put to the test on the level of culture and ideas. The person who enters will be confronted with generations very different from his own. How will he live with that difference of age, culture and practices of life? This can be a great challenge, both for the candidate and for the persons in charge of his formation.

Newcomers should thus be formed to manage their freedom with the help of the institutional framework which is offered them. At the same time, the existing framework should not become a crutch the individual cannot do without. It should be a positive element that helps the candidate to develop his personality. To accept a rule, the practice of certain observances, the sometimes invasive and especially inquisitive curiosity of a community, is a situation which is not easy for anybody accustomed to his own autonomy. Persons in charge of formation have an important role to present the positive aspects of this new situation. The structure can support the frailty of the person if he can use it with flexibility and understanding. "To be flexible" does not mean "to abandon requirements." However, at the same time, firmness presupposes benevolent and human guidance. Firmness must come more from the person himself rather than from the person in charge of formation. It is necessary to train men and women of character. It is necessary to educate the will.

Detachment from close relatives and friends

We often underestimate much of the emotional load brought on by a drastic change from a candidate's previous life environment. The professional man or the laborer who switches careers takes with him his wife, his children, and easily goes back to his paternal home. He re-establishes his friendships without difficulty. He meets his former colleagues from work. Courage is needed today to leave all that the world has to offer in order to become part of a regulated life apart from all that had been previously known. What does it mean to leave that familiar "visual environment," the multiple activities, the friends and the parents who are not there any more to share your life? Experiencing a departure especially frightens older people. To move away from those whom one loves is distressing for any person who has a heart.

We are all afraid of losing something forever. This is why I insist on the "desire" for detachment in religious life. Religious life requires detachment and that is very difficult for most. Communities don't always understand the fracture that takes place on the psychological level. Friends or parents write, update, suggest and sometimes hope for a return. Friends marry, change profession, and make plans without us. Marriages are announced, as well as the births of children, planned vacations, deaths. Separation from all this can cause suffering. Will there be something equally attractive in our communities so that the person chooses to remain there in spite of the temptation of going back to the past? It is important for the person in charge of formation – and also the community – to think about that. Here, the relationship with Christ is very important. Only the love of Christ and the salvation of others can really explain such a separation. The community must offer a way of life which captivates the candidate's interest. Individualism and the absence of communal activities can generate a certain sadness and compound the sense of emptiness which a departure can cause. One went from a period of no-choice to one of the integration of his choice.

> Insofar as he who embraces a religious state of life moves completely away from his former environment, or shows a certain distance with respect to it, this same environment then loses a member who belonged to it. In what relates to him, he seems to some extent deprived of a right and that is indeed the case. A vacuum is created, and the question arises of knowing how to make the best of it.[37]

The person goes through a time of strange relationship with his or her new environment. All is new, the habits of life, the buildings, and the surroundings. New interests have to become their own. It is necessary that they remember the reasons which guided them in this desire to give themselves to the Lord. "Why am I here? What did I come to do in this house of obedience and way of humility?" In adapting to this new environment, they may well lose their thirst and desire to go on. The mind often plays a dissuasive role regarding their choice. They remember friends, parents, leisure time activities and especially their past freedom. Sometimes, they are inclined to let it all go. This period can be very difficult and discourages many. The person in charge of formation has the responsibility to be sensitive and to listen attentively in order to support the candidate's perseverance. It is through constant prayer to God that their choice will be strengthened. At this point in time it is good to recall the reasons that led to this paradoxical situation which is the religious life.

The community also has a role to play. I will come back to this topic when I touch on the subject of the formation community. For the first two years of initial formation, it is desirable to avoid visits to the family, without however limiting the visits to the community on the part of parents and friends. Their coming can attenuate the sense of loneliness and loss.

Work and self-realization

In the world, we choose a career, a work place. We have control over the rhythm of our life. It is not the same with a community. What can it offer us now or in the future? The situation is not very clear at the time of entrance. What will be the means at our disposal to get satisfaction out of our apostolate or out of life itself? What will be the scope of our freedom of action? In a convent or monastery, where can we find the possibility to grow in spite of the daily routine? What will be the directions?

All these questions will gradually find answer as the person familiarizes him or herself with the environment, and progresses in religious life.

By virtue of the simple fact of one's astonishment and surprise, one does not have to start carrying out a routine lifestyle where he is satisfied with following along without reacting internally, where he seeks to integrate everything and to master everything as quickly as possible, by immediately adopting new clothing and, though still a beginner, trying to keep pace with the master even before having understood anything.

This constitutes the greatest danger for beginners: to integrate everything but in a global and superficial way, precisely because of the multitude of impressions which are offered to them. These impressions are part of the new state of life, but they need to be internally assimilated, separately, successively, and not all at the same time. For it is not a question of a training exercise, but of an answer addressed to God by a Christian who made a choice. One is likely to put on an equal footing – and consequently to confuse – the external life – the rule of the house, the daily timetable – with the essence, the interior life; in other words, to try to assimilate the appearance so quickly that one forgets to take care of the interior aspect. Nor should one, at the beginning, want to take the best; he should rather be satisfied with what is given. Some feel embarrassment at being very young grooms or brand new seminarians; they would rather not be seen; they would prefer to disappear immediately. But this can only lead to failure.[38]

It takes time for fear to wear off through the interaction between adaptation to community life and growth in the interior life. The aim of the religious, especially during the novitiate, is to cultivate a relationship with God, to learn how to listen to His Word. The discipline of life is there to support this progress. Candidates will pay attention to the petty rules which do nothing but disturb them and their interior growth. Flexibility will enable them to overcome their fears and anxieties. Here both the person in charge of formation and the community have a crucial role to play in order to put priorities in the right place. The interior life must take precedence over external behavior.

However, today people require structure so they will not feel lost.

> The new environment can, at first sight, appear so strange that a person feels lost, so to speak. However, he cannot constantly keep looking back, taking everything along with himself like an old acquaintance, his own self; he must set his heart and intelligence on this new reality, in order to discover in it the plenitude of significance that God offers him through it. Any partial demands must be considered in the light of the great overall requirement; a "yes" to God can be divided into as many parts as one wants. This "yes" however always remains a whole.[39]

Observances, Habits, feasts, meetings, and community work reinforce a bond with the community and create an attachment to it. Community responsibilities help the newcomer become rooted in the community. Especially regarding their studies, students need not become "first class scholars" whose sole universe would revolve around their books. The risk would be to train people with unrealistic illusions. Small responsibilities make it possible to avoid infantilism. It is necessary to arrive at the right proportion of emotional investment in each sector of life: manual work, leisure, studies, prayer, solitude, silence, apostolate, and external contacts. The interior human being is not developed in activism and dispersion.

First Challenges

The place of formation

Today's young people are very little accustomed to living with others. As we said earlier, smaller families promote a certain individualism. Children are protected from character and personality shock. Now they must get accustomed to life in a group. In a progressive way, a relationship is established with the person in charge of formation, then with one or two other people in the community. In time, these relationships open out and become plural. At this point in time the person finds his happiness. Here pops up one of the great challenges to communities in our time. How to help those accustomed to individualism develop a group spirit?

This challenge shows up under various forms, from one community to another, and from one type of religious life to another.

For contemplative communities, the "elbow to elbow" situation is more intense and external contact is reduced to a minimum. This proximity presents a real difficulty. Young people find themselves in the monastery with adults who could be their parents. Recruitment is done individually and the average age is high. The beginner is often alone with the master of formation because of the separation of the novitiate from the community.

Too often we have hesitated to correct this situation. The

argument brought forward has been the need for a formation in the monastery where the candidate is willing to engage himself. However "the good" of the person in formation is partly over-shadowed. There is a kind of blindness vis-à-vis reality. Once a monastic nun said to me, "What is destroying us today is pride." Perhaps she was not wrong. We yielded under the pressure of our communities so that each monastery could keep its autonomy. In my humble opinion, that is no longer possible in our century. New formulas for formation have been put forward in a number of countries and these experiences of collaboration have showed the logic of a regrouping of individuals rather than their disper-sion. We are likely to sacrifice monastic life because of formulas which made sense when monasteries recruited in great numbers. Each one of them could support an adequate training for its members. For many monasteries now, that is no longer possible. The lack of vocations demands a new approach.

The context is different for apostolic religious communities. There, too, we find hesitation when faced with innovation. There are more and more difficulties finding religious to accompany candidates in formation. When one succeeds in forming a group or a community, the differences in ages and mentalities are such that it is not any more very easy to provide newcomers with a balanced environment.

At the same time, we hesitate to entrust our candidates to other younger and better organized institutional entities. Often, cultural or ideological reasons block certain initiatives. It is nec-essary to dare to take risks and not to be afraid of sending our candidates to be formed where things are going well. Admittedly, mentalities, as well as customs and habits, will be different from one country to another, but the important thing is to give a basic training of quality and to do it in a group. In any case, each generation must invent its own dynamism and learn how to integrate themselves in different groups throughout life. Let us not be too concerned about perpetuating ourselves in them. The media engages us in a new cultural and social dynamic. Communities must likewise be accustomed to these blends of culture.

Confrontation of generations or "inter-generation"

Teachings are necessary, but are not sufficient to prepare one for community life. The master has the task to help "put words" to the experience. Thus the dialogue between the master and the disciple should promote reflection, encouraging the candidate to put things in perspective. The master's advice allows the candidate to clarify his experience and to look objectively at various situations.

But adaptation is a process which develops especially through interaction with those of the same generation, living the same experience. How many religious vocations have been lost because of isolation from people of their own generation? For apostolic communities, this situation is dramatic because loneliness has led to an internal counter-culture which maintains a conflict between generations. The inclination is to recall many past difficulties and to choose one option over another without having tried out the beauty of a rich community life of feelings and emotions lived elbow to elbow.

Too often in certain communities a "dad/mom dynamic" settles in. Newcomers are excluded for years, becoming "insignificant persons" who succeed in being integrated into the system only after passing through a number of tests. Endurance comes to be the first gift of grace, but weaker or more fragile persons are often at risk, trying to walk in another person's shoes as it were.

Sometimes they give up, disillusioned by events and situations. Their decision to leave is not always a mature one. Doubt lingers on and their departures leave a bad taste.

Surely, candidates should not be put into intolerable situations of conflict. They need to be comforted and supported. Thus, the composition of communities of formation plays a very important role. But to seek the perfect community is not necessary. As good religious as we may be, we remain human beings.

A method of formation and a structure of life

Adaptation to religious life must be done with method and discipline. A choice has been made. From now on the candidate must enter into a pattern of life in which they are a partner. They do not enter a vise, but rather a process where they will be the principal agents of their own formation.

Any community has observances, customs, and ways of doing things. Religious life is an institutional life which structures the individuals, thus supporting their training in view of the apostolate and the life of the community. The environment must allow for a progressive comprehension of the need for observances. This is not an aim in itself, but a means towards the service of a goal: union with God and charity towards neighbor in the contemplative or apostolic life.

The community must avoid dogmatizing their practices and customs which often do not have anything to do with the quality of religious life. In fact, they can often be obstacles to adaptation. Frequently, theories, personal opinions or attitudes are raised to the rank of laws, impossible to circumvent, weighing heavily on newcomers. They cannot understand these requirements which often seem irrelevant to the culture of their generation. Here are some examples: "Orange juice for breakfast every day is a whim and is too expensive." "It is against religious poverty to keep our buildings this warm." "Why put in central heating when we could be doing penance and realize the savings?" "We should drink our coffee from a bowl; it's the custom of our congregation, and our founders all did it." "The poor don't have computers; then, why do we have them?" "One should not cross their legs." And you could go on and on. It would be a never-ending list.

Seen in their symbolic meaning, practices are an excellent way to give body to spirituality and to develop identity. They can be very nasty if they are imposed on the members and do not coincide with the goodwill of each one to observe them. They must help to structure the members and not to impose on them unimportant and cumbersome lifestyles. Many observances promote a sense of belonging to the group and tangibly manifest the communion of the members. They should be based on a strong and well-balanced spiritual life inasmuch as they make the members happy internally. They should not lead to exaggerations or affected "mannerisms." An example: times of silence can be sources of reflection and peace in the community. Silence can likewise help promote a sense of interiority. But a meddlesome and too lengthy silence can bring about a climate of tension, capable of exacerbating more fragile personalities. If there is no place in our communities for the weakest, shouldn't we raise questions about the evangelic value of the religious life? The Rule of Saint Benedict and the Rule of Saint Augustine clearly specify that it is necessary to hold ourselves accountable for the health and well-being of each one. In certain communities, exaggeratedly meticulous and demanding observances are coming back. However the upcoming generations seem to appreciate the esoteric aspect of these customs; I see two dangers here.

Numerous and intruding practices can weaken the will to persevere as well as one's psychological equilibrium. This is the first danger. Through dogged determination, a member obeys the rules and sees that as progress. In the long run, what appears to be a victory over the ego turns into a quest for personal aggrandizement. A disproportionate link is established between the will and the spiritual life. Initially it may seem like a grace from God. But the more one progresses, the more it becomes a yoke and a burden, as Jesus says. Then failure discourages, and one turns pessimistic. Confidence in God wanes. Formation must bring the person to regularity of observances. But the goal is not this regularity. The obligation must always be subjected to charity. It must cause confidence and not magnify weakness.

The second danger is to subject the person to a yoke that Christ himself did not want to force upon us. In these circumstances, we then judge a vocation on endurance rather than on grace, on the will rather than on love, on aptitudes rather than on faith. We are challenged here by the hope that Christ put in us: that observance should be at the service of the religious and not the religious at the service of observance! Those who are successful for a few years sometimes impose their will on more fragile members. These latter are also called by Christ to follow Him.

> Come unto me, all you who labor and are heavy burdened, and I will give you rest. Take my yoke upon you, and learn from me; for I am meek and lowly of heart: and you shall find rest for your souls, for my yoke is easy, and my burden is light.[40]

The "yoke" represents God's Law. How could we impose, in our manner of living, that from which Jesus came to free us. If obedience to the Law, lived as a sacrifice, remains a creditable method of purification of the will and of the heart, making an absolute of it would amount to reassuming the "burden" that Jesus wanted to remove. A discipline of life should certainly be acquired by the imitation and the repetition of gestures. A fixed order of the day develops practices of regular life. But through this repetition of gestures and words, the person is meant to acquire the will to persevere for a greater spiritual and human good. It is the role of education to convince us of the value of the effort to arrive at a goal. But this effort should never be to the detriment of a healthy notion of faith. Saint Paul's words invite us to think of the end towards which we walk.

> Not that I've already achieved this [goal – to know Christ and the power of his resurrection] or that I'm already perfect! But I continue to strive in the hope of making it my own, because Christ Jesus has made me his own. My brothers, I don't consider that I've won yet, and for this reason I forget what's behind me and reach out for what's in front of me. I strain toward the goal to win the prize of God's heavenward call in Christ Jesus. So let us who are mature adopt this attitude, and if your attitude is otherwise, God will reveal this to you as well. But let us conduct ourselves in the light of what we've already attained. [41]

Let us walk in the same direction in communion with each other. Let us help each other along the way. Paul is conscious that grace enabled him to make choices. He is thus ready to make all the required effort to walk in the right direction. For us, religious, the framework of life must enable us to move forward just as Paul encourages us to do. However, without a precise object, the framework would only be one way of disciplining ourselves. On the contrary, our way of living as religious must be the means par excellence which leads to God. Just like Paul, religious are gradually seized by grace and walk courageously while devoting themselves completely to the actualization of the life of Christ in themselves. The purpose of our observances is precisely this race towards the achievement of our vocation which is to follow Christ until the moment of our identification with Him becomes perfect. It is our faith which comes to nourish our personal convictions. It is not our observances which nourish our faith. Observances only provide a framework so that all our energy is devoted to listening to the Lord.

The work

Formerly, in apostolic religious communities, the effectiveness of the apostolate was rated first in importance. Community life could get second rank among priorities. People, and their prayer life, were often sacrificed to the service of the Institution or the apostolate. Nuns often became institutionalized women, to the detriment of their spiritual life. Some no longer manage to control the amount of work required to maintain their buildings and to earn a living. This can be demoralizing for somebody who wants to enter religious life. How can we find a balance between the desire to maintain an old lifestyle and monastic tradition amid today's apostolic workload? Here the role of the superiors is very important. What orientation will they give to their communities? What burdens will be imposed upon the shoulders of the young who aspire to religious life? The spiritual life cannot develop in a climate of tension and hyperactivity. "Mission at all costs" does not have its place in religious life. We will have to descend from our high ideals to find a more human ground on which to evolve and where one will be able to live better.

Work in the secular world is a means of earning a living or realizing one's potential. Some invest a lot of energy in that. This will for self-realization gains importance in apostolic religious communities. The older members still have an acute sense of duty. The method of formation must take into account this need for self-realization. Work can be an asceticism helping to achieve a better sense of community. It must also allow for the use of a member's talents and acquired skills. Formation should not exclude the possibility of satisfying a person's preferences through the work assigned in continuity with past experience. Right at the beginning of formation, especially in apostolic communities, after the canonical year of novitiate, one should not hesitate to entrust responsibilities to the young religious.

Work is an activity where the person in charge of formation can check on the behavior of the candidate and help him to grow in evangelical holiness. It is here that advice and support can give direction to the work. While this advice is certainly connected to reality it is also connected to the charism of the institute. It thus provides an occasion for the young religious to share with the person in charge of formation his hopes, his disappointments, the difficulties he has with one or another member, the reasons for any delay in his community and apostolic integration. Through work, tomorrow's religious takes shape and is built up as a spiritual and apostolic being.

Let us not consider religious in formation as workers for all the jobs that others do not like to do. A newcomer is easily baffled by the lack of consideration on the part of his or her elders about the kind of work that they entrust to them.

For some, religious life often causes a regression to teenage attitudes. At the age at which candidates enter today, we should not hesitate to entrust adult tasks to them. We should not confuse "the spiritual childhood" of Thérèse de Lisieux with "infantilism" whose effects would cause a regression to a childish state. In the apostolate, the presence of elders can be useful in supporting pastoral growth. But this mentor is not located at the level of the authority. He is there rather to support the acquisition of skills and to develop the aptitudes of the candidate. He represents "big brother's guiding hand." His presence and his fraternal attention should lead to a healthy autonomy.

Precise and verifiable objectives

The formation program, as well as the person in charge of formation, must propose precise short- and long-term objectives. All must be clear about the objectives to be pursued.

The person in charge of formation must always prepare stages, in order to note, at their conclusion, if the intended aims are realistic. These stages provide the occasion to see whether what has been asked of the candidate falls well within the objectives of the community. Each member follows a very personal path but always in relation to the community. The interaction mainly occurs between the person in charge of formation and the candidate, but the entire community of formation plays a formative role. The candidate, however, should not feel inhibited by the presence of too many actors.

Everything does not fall under the exclusive domain of the master of formation. Formation is done mainly through osmosis and dialogue. Candidates run the risk of feeling completely oppressed by a system of formation that is too tense and too demanding. It is necessary to give formation a peaceful rhythm. This is what guarantees a serene evolution. Otherwise, interpersonal relationships can become very conflictive and the candidate could develop behaviors that he or she would not develop in a normal situation. Religious tend to consider newcomers too severely, to judge them and often to impose on them their point of view. They forget that they are of another generation. The person in charge of formation must manage the relationship between the community and the candidate to avoid misunderstandings. Here, the community has the responsibility to give their confidence to the person in charge of formation.

Adaptation is done step by step, taking into account the various successes. It is by this autonomy that one develops an adult attitude. By repeating the same gestures and the same ways of doing, one will come to develop a habit. Successes will be an incentive to go forward on the path. Let us emphasize positive forms of behavior so that the person becomes more trustful and discovers that he or she is able to initiate activities and to conclude them on their own. Coherent means and possible choices lead to a fulfilling life. That implies temporary renunciations in order to achieve the ultimate goal.

The person in charge of formation must regularly discuss with the candidate what has been lived. At the time of the interview, successes are underlined and failures are put into perspective. It is easy to concentrate on difficulties whereas it is advisable to see them as springboards towards better results. This type of reflection can remind the person what they wanted to achieve in the context of their commitment. "You want to become a religious, you gave yourself a precise goal, a challenge, you want to become a cloistered religious, you want to become contemplative or apostolic religious in the line of such or such a charism, then, in view of this very general objective, what leads you to success on such or such a point?" Taking into account the objective, we must re-examine the success according to the commitment and see with the person how he or she got there. Finally, it is necessary to move attention off the objective and examine what the person experienced and why he or she made such and such a decision, and what means were used. The person then becomes conscious of the sacrifice that had to be made to arrive at this point. He or she acquires greater confidence in self and are able to distance themselves from their acts.

In this way one's personal and religious identity is constructed. What appeared impossible becomes possible. The person builds on positive experiences. The values are incarnated when there is experience in a lived context which gives a sense of direction to the endeavor.

The sense of the authority

A relationship with authority develops insofar as the person in charge of formation is able to combine kindness with the demands of religious life. The spirit of obedience can only grow if the judgment of the superior is confident and enlightened.

Generally, it is necessary to avoid making decisions too hastily where matters would be handled without much discernment. On the other hand, the candidate will feel confident if the person in charge of formation is able to make decisions without hesitation while keeping a great spirit of humility. The person in charge of formation can be mistaken at times; he or she must recognize this.

People agree on a certain degree of collegial direction. But they are embarrassed by interminable discussions in the name of democracy on points or details of no importance. Long debates can lead to psychological fatigue, making people feel insecure. While wishing that problems be handled promptly it should not be expected that those in charge always have an opinion for or against everything. Dialogue and exchange are appropriate and appreciated insofar as the objectives are worth the effort.

When I was in formation, the community could not accept a minor change in the timetable and our way of living. The least change was seen as a big problem. To change the time for the recitation of the Office was a major event! It took many years to adjust the time of the recitation by fifteen minutes. I had already left formation for a long time when the decision was finally made. It was too late to benefit from it. It is very difficult for young people to hear: "We've always done it that way!" or: "A consensus should be reached." There are things which are objective realities. Very often in community, a habit can be developed of always expressing the opposite opinion to a proposal. "We can't because…" It is often necessary to decide according to the common good and not always according to a consensus. Sometimes it is necessary to decide in favor of our young people. How painful it is for them to always have to justify the least desire and to feel a constant opposition from older members. The master of formation must be able to manage the differences in points of view between the elders and the young. Often, he will find it difficult to justify certain attitudes of the elders. He must discuss this in an honest way even when it may put him in disagreement with the community. But he must always remind everyone of the duty of obedience and compassion.

Decisions cannot always satisfy everyone's sensibility. Here, superiors have an essential role to play in not letting disagreements undermine the atmosphere of a community. The law of consensus is often the law of the lowest common denominator. There is then the risk of sinking into mediocrity. The person in charge of formation and the superior must aim at exerting their authority with prudence but without falling into inaction. There would be much more to say on the functioning of our communities. Meetings are largely useful in learning how to share on points which cause embarrassment or uneasiness. These exchanges can help with formation through healthy dialogue. They allow for clearing up the frustrations caused by small dissatisfactions.

Training in obedience

No one can adapt to what he does not know. Vague and imprecise objectives sow confusion and sometimes mistrust. It is necessary that the candidates know what the community expects from them. Imprecise and unclear ideas hide the true object of formation and especially of religious life. Disagreements often come about owing to the fact that there is no unanimity regarding the community project. Within a democratic framework, inaccuracies, doubts and multiple hesitations obstruct the adaptation. A community which argues about everything, without determining matters in a precise way, is likely to maintain constant disagreement. Obedience is exerted after open discussion, honest proposals and a clear decision-making process which concludes the debate. Newcomers must learn how to live with decisions contrary to their own ideas. Proposals must be welcomed as the work of the Holy Spirit in each member.

These conclusions will be better accepted when we understand that nothing is immutable and that everything can be called into question at a later date. One of the difficulties of the community process is the impression that the decisions are made for an indefinite period of time without any possibility, after some experience, to reconsider the question. If the members of a community agree on a later re-evaluation, all will more easily agree to accept the decision.

Here, sticking with the Constitutions can foster unity. Interpretations that are too fuzzy and too personal are likely to destroy the enthusiasm of newcomers with regard to the relevance of the rule and the Constitutions. We train young people for the community and not for us. It is their hope to follow Christ that counts. It is not the ideas of everyone that define a formation plan or community project. We cannot adapt to the wishes of every one. We adapt to an environment, a specific work, a precise lifestyle. Otherwise, confusion and discouragement install themselves. We welcome adults; and the difficulty of obedience can be very challenging. Here, Dom Ducruet, O.S.B., enlightens us:

> Each age has its own way to obey, to come of age and to open up to the other's mystery while responding to the questions that the other poses to us. Each life has its own age of maturity. That of a five-year-old child is not that of a twenty-year-old young person, nor that of a forty-year-old man. But there is always something common to all ages, viz. to obey, beyond the order given, to the person's conscience enlightened by the Holy Spirit. There is always a personal and theological dimension to full and mature obedience.[42]

Formation must be a stage where training leads to maturity thanks to a program and to objectives clearly showing the route to follow. Obedience is initially learned by the cogency and objectivity of the requirements. It is embedded in a dialogue. The pursuit of personal objectives comes to help the candidate to grow, all the while being aware of the needs of the community. The Holy Spirit works hand in hand with the motivation of people, the expectations of institutions and the environments that the religious chooses for his progress.

What we ask must take into account the situation of the community and of the individual as well as the progress already reached. The act of obedience is always located in a very concrete context lived with others. The humility that leads to obedience is not humiliation which leads to servility. He who obeys must be able to keep his dignity, preserving his opinion about himself. It is necessary to avoid making someone "*lose face*"!

In the event of disagreement, it should not be expected that the individual be disavowed. He or she must obey, but without being obliged to change their opinion on such or such point. Moreover, it should not be asked that the candidates decide by themselves under the pretext of helping to form their freedom without initially clearly expressing the needs of the community and the Church. Superiors must assume their own responsibilities and not put on their subordinates' shoulders what falls on them to decide. A certain theory of government suggests that obedience is the result of the meeting of two wills in the act of obeying. This is desirable, but is not always possible. When somebody is confronted with multiple requests and is under pressure to make a choice, he or she must feel that they are supported in this process. It may be for them a calling into question something which displeases them or causes them a difficulty. A re-examination will make it possible to note that the wisdom of the superiors allows for some progress on the human and spiritual levels which one had not thought of. In cases of doubt on behalf of the person concerned, those in charge of formation or the superiors should not hesitate to make those decisions which come under their own responsibilities. If they are mistaken, it is then up to them to reconsider their decisions.

Religious must comply with the rules of civility and overcome a certain relaxation in the way they deal with relationships! Young people who enter have been active in the market place; they are accustomed to accept positive and satisfactory observations about already concluded work or behavior. To be able and to dare to say: "Thank you! That is beautiful! That is good!" is know-how that humanizes the relationship between the members of a community. At a certain age, adapting one's personality becomes more difficult. People should be accepted as they are. It is necessary to open up to differences. Young people must also accept diversity. This does not always come easy for them. Gradually, the person in charge of formation must bring the candidate to a better comprehension of differences and to patience vis-à-vis his or her expectations. Here, the sensitivity of each one plays a big role in formation, and some self-control must be inculcated.

Some have entered apostolic communities where they could not stay simply because someone tried to give them a label, in the name of the spirituality or of the charism, which they could not accept. Often we say that we want to welcome younger candidates because they are so flexible. Nothing proves this assertion to be true. Shouldn't we reflect a little more on this question? For more or less fifty years now, many religious have left our ranks. The majority of them were people who had entered at a very young age and who were supposedly "flexible." We have to be careful not to disregard these many departures.

To refuse to admit older candidates for fear of non-adaptation would amount to saying that the person has to adopt the mould that is imposed on them, be they young or not so young. The work of the Holy Spirit then would be underestimated as well as the potential creativity and goodwill of the candidates themselves. Within this fear of maladjustment isn't there a hidden desire to want to impose a certain manner of being? Let us not try to reproduce photocopied portraits of what we are. Respecting the individual leads to good adjustment and to love of self and of others. It is not easy for the young people who come in. Youthful as they are, they enter with personalities already structured by an environment completely foreign to our way of seeing things. Any person who chooses religious life today knows that he has a long path to follow in order to arrive at sanctity. Jesus gave to all those who followed Him the chance to progress in faith. Shouldn't we also give them a try? It is the convergence of two desires which we have to work on. The community must accommodate those who enter by looking at them positively. On the other hand, those who enter must accept those who are already there as they are, and grow with them.

Training on the move and the dynamics of integration

Formation must be part of a progressive movement towards greater adjustment. It must, of course, provide a framework. This framework helps to structure the personality of the future religious on the cultural, spiritual, intellectual and apostolic levels. But it is a movement of life which helps the religious to progress towards the spiritual being he or she wants to become:

> It then appears clearly that to be the mirror of God, the Christian life needs an interior dynamism. The states of life, such as they are shaped by the Church, constitute, each one in its way, a life in motion to which an individual must give his agreement. It is only in this way that one will be able to understand that a man, who said yes to a state of life, can persevere in it during his whole life. From the very point of view

of the faith, this would be impossible for him if this yes to a state of life were not flexible and mobile, and if, in his being, there were no foreseeable evolution. If the man were to say yes to a state that would be only a static situation, this would be for him a way of burying himself alive. But for God, life is inscribed in His eternal being, whereas for us, our being depends on its evolution. However, in order that we remain alive within our state of life, it is necessary that this state receives its dynamism from God. Vitality comes from God; it is communicated to the state of life which must accommodate it. The eternal dynamism of God is also transmitted to the state of life in the form of movement. Divine vitality does not solidify at the time of this transmission. It preserves, in the grace of the state of life, the ability to partake in the eternal life.[43]

One of the difficulties of current religious communities resides in the fact that their members wish that the people who enter be on the same level as themselves culturally, spiritually and humanly. That is impossible because of the differences in generations. Hence, we have to let the benefits of the Word of God who impregnates the mentality of each one at different rhythms come to life in the candidates. The role of the person in charge of formation is very important here, since he or she becomes the privileged agent who, in their exchanges with the candidate, can gradually make things progress and fit into the developmental scheme of the individual. One should not go more quickly than grace, and it is necessary to leave "time to time," as the proverb goes. We should neither precipitate things, nor let them go. Good judgment about a candidate falls under the dynamics of a formative community. It takes a whole life to become a saint. We must realize that, for ourselves as well as for others. We need a lifetime to mature and become fully human. Each lifespan carries particular dynamics connected to it. There is a time for everything under the sun. Let us try to help the Holy Spirit accomplish His work and especially to take His proper place. Let us allow others to become what they are called and meant to be.

A clarification: For young people coming from a very individualistic environment, formation to community life is very difficult. They need space to express their individualism, even if it is very difficult to manage. They should not be expected to always be together in rank and file. To have coffee with one another, or to go for a walk together, is a matter of the healthy management of relationships. It takes time to feel at ease with everyone.

We need time, alone or in small group, to assimilate relationships with the many people around us.

The person vis-à-vis his new environment

We should go deeper into this concept of discretion previously mentioned. Confidence can exist only with the certainty of the discretion on the part of the person in charge of formation. Conscience remains a private domain. For the person in charge of formation, it is difficult, because fellow-members are inquisitive. They get worried. They want to know. But there is a danger in allowing certain members of the community into confidence. It is necessary to be very careful. To speak too much is to risk revealing an individual's privacy.

Newcomers must accept things they will not be in agreement with. Too many observations regarding the internal dynamics of the community can create fixations. In the outside world, people do not always do what they want. By entering a community, they enter a structured and protected environment.

VOCATIONS AND THEIR FORMATION TODAY

They might think that everything would happen smoothly. It is not always understood that if they were to go back to where they came from, all would not be ideal either. Married, with children, would life be more "glowing"? Each state of life has its own specific dynamics, its joys and imperfections. The important thing is to find our place and adapt to it. Let us give ourselves time to put things in perspective. What makes it possible for a family to appreciate being together is their mutual love and gift of self to one another. The same is true for a community; it is love that leads to the acceptance of our differences.

The question of elderly religious is a big preoccupation for many in their communities. When young people say to me that they are afraid to have to support the elderly members for the remainder of their lives, I say this to them: "You, too, one day, will be old or sick." In the current world, social institutions encourage people to hide real suffering and to ignore illness and death. In this case, by their very presence, the community has to be a witness to declining patients and elderly people. Young people are open to community solidarity. Formation can support this attitude of compassion for the aged and the weak. Our apostolic ministry or work is no excuse to forget those who suffer inside our walls. Our "first neighbor" is the one with whom we chose to spend the remainder of our lives. The parable of the Good Samaritan points out the importance of becoming a neighbor to one another. Here, we do not have to imitate today's society's ways of doing things, which has so institutionalized the health care system that patients are often forgotten in their loneliness. Religious life is the narrow path which helps its members to take on a profound evangelical spirit.

When someone enters a religious community, he leaves behind a familiar milieu. Here he no longer chooses his neighbors.

Neighbors? It is the community, they are our brothers, our sisters, whatever their age, health and character. And this should be made clear in such a manner that newcomers become aware of it.

Let us add that sports and legitimate leisure time support physical as well as psychological growth. Reading, walking, and the arts – especially painting, sculpture and listening to music – are other means of maturing in community. The monastic environment must be a true living space where an individual finds inside the walls of the religious house all that is necessary for psychological and physical equilibrium. In this way, he or she can support the daily burden of communal life. For the apostolic religious, any internal commitment in community work, in the management of the community and its apostolate, allows a significant insertion which facilitates the adaptation of the newcomer without being in opposition to the external apostolate. Then they are no longer tempted to look at the community as external to themselves, judging it from a critical perspective; but on the contrary, they understand it from the inside. Religious in formation are not boarders but full members.

To present a vision with a future

The means that we propose for formation must match the personal aspirations of the candidate, and the community must propose a vision with a future. Past traditions are not enough to motivate newcomers. Projects can be along the historical lines of the community and its charism. But these projects must constantly be evaluated, updated and revitalized. A new formulation of objectives and new ways of doing things encourage newcomers to involve themselves in the phases of community evolution. However, other projects will be created to answer new needs, to make something "new." To make something new does not always mean to found new communities. To make something new can also mean to make existing projects evolve.

Young people do not want to enter an environment that would constantly be called into question and that would constantly waver about its future. A person's life project must be clear and justified. Then they will not hesitate to be more involved, especially as they are recognized for their contribution. Young people expect that we propose something which requires a certain radicalism and the gift of self. However, that supposes that the elders make a place for them and do not seek to monopolize all the tasks and the decisions.

Two types of people enter our communities. There are those who will be more or less satisfied with what already exists and they will simply want to collaborate to maintain it. Others will have a more creative spirit and will wish to make use of it. Those in charge of formation and the superiors must be attentive in detecting these personality types and in giving each of them the opportunity to develop their talents. Every one needs to feel that he or she has positive value in the community.

In the past, there existed a spirituality of *"detachment."* It was necessary to be ready to live in a changing situation. This is all very beautiful when you have a safety net to protect yourself in the event of difficulties. It is the language of people who have all they need. It is the language of the rich. When I was in formation, a fellow-member retorted: "We are not yet settled down. Give us time to get there, before disturbing us!" This spirituality of *"detachment"* is praiseworthy from an evangelical point of view. But there is a time for everything in life. Jesus disturbs us. But He also gives reassurance. Jesus' speech was coherent. It offered something which represented a stable objective with precise points of reference. It is important for everyone to spend a certain amount of time being devoted to a cause. Following profession will be time enough to be troubled if the occasion presents itself and if the will is there. However, religious in formation will first have to learn a certain mobility. One thing at a time.

Emotional life and sexuality

One who decides to enter a community should be aware of the impact that separation will have on his emotional life. He joins an environment where a person's emotional life will occasionally be disturbed and where he will live in denial of his sexual instincts. To be unaware of that would be to take the risk of becoming emotionally unbalanced or a too sensitive psychopath. A long period of maturation will be necessary in order for a person to be happy living side by side with others which, in a certain sense, goes contrary to nature. When a person is married and in love, he lives close to his wife and children in a developing relationship; even though this proximity is sometimes difficult. The required effort is rewarded by a feeling of happiness and well-being. Religious life does not always offer this compensation. The mission and its joys do not always fill the emotional vacuum.

Today, emotional maturity is often spoken about.

There is no maturity in and by itself. It varies according to age, people, marital statuses, states of life and cultures. Abrupt changes in our lives can deeply deteriorate the maturity that one assumed he had reached.[44]

This is a piece of profound realism. This same General Chapter declared:

There is no maturity without personal autonomy, resulting from an awakening and knowledge of oneself. Through the stages of our human life, we learn, on the one hand, to keep a right distance compared to the strains and questionings coming from outside and, on the other hand, to develop a capacity to accept them and to take them into account.[45]

It is important to note the fragility of the people who suddenly reorient their lives to devote themselves to God. They do so with all their affectivity and their sexuality. The sexual instinct is then seen as being withheld.

Too often, we avoid mentioning the word "sexuality." Perhaps it's too explicit for our ears. But let us be realistic. Those who enter today's communities often have had previous sexual relations. They have engaged in acts of intimacy. To find yourself among persons of the same sex in a relationship of equal to equal, without knowing each other, after having received a very different education, is not easy for the person who enters a group already formed. This group already has its practices, taboos, ideas, points of reference, silences, linguistic codes, ways of thinking, and concepts of community life and apostolate. The view of the world and society differs from one person to the next. The members of the community have already formed friendships. They have already established grounds of agreement and they already know the triggers of arguments which they can avoid.

For the newcomer, all these things are still foreign to him. He will gradually have to discover and assimilate them in a sometimes frustrating and long process of integration. Those who have more difficulty in integrating will sometimes feel themselves judged. We should not expect perfect integration before several years have passed. We are not a "club of well-balanced individuals." We are an association of sinners. Love, in the sense of "charity," must guide our adaptation. It is necessary to give chances and the person in charge of formation must have a free hand in this field. He must be able to work with the person in a discrete way and without interference.

> Let us not think that all will unfold well if we recruit balanced young men and women, free of any apparent emotional disorder. Would balanced people give their lives for their friends? Would they leave the ninety ewes to go and seek that which was mislaid? Would they drink and eat with prostitutes and sinners? I am very afraid that they would be too reasonable. Commenting on the Gospel according to Saint John, Saint Augustine wrote "Show me somebody who loves: he understands what I am saying" (Jn 17:26). Only those who are capable of love will be able to understand the passion of the apostolic life. If we do not let ourselves be carried by the wave of this immense love, all our attempts to be pure could well end in control exercises. We may succeed there, but with the risk of doing great damage to ourselves. We can fail, with the risk of causing terrible wrongs to our neighbor.[46]

Formation in chastity requires a lengthy apprenticeship. Only time strengthens the will. Those in charge of formation must be open enough to listen and to understand. He must guide the person in a way that moves him forward to a greater ease and a greater comprehension of his life in relation to others. Frank and honest dialogue, in a climate of confidence, must be established between the person in charge of formation and the religious in formation. If this is not the case, one should not hesitate to entrust the novice to the care of another with whom he will be more at ease. He needs to be able to speak about the emotional aspects of his life.

Prayer and dialogue come to play a very important role here. Prayer, *lectio divina*, meditation on the Word of God coupled with a rule of life, are means which allow "an inner detachment necessary for maturation."[47] Slowly the conversion of heart takes place and the union with God increases. Then community life with one's brothers can really support the individual in difficult times. Dialogue takes its rightful place, especially with the master of formation. This also helps and supports an individual vis-à-vis the uncertainties and discouragements he may encounter.

The apostolate supports this commitment of emotional life to the service of the Church and the community. As long as there is a missionary motivation, chastity is possible. In paying attention to our neighbor, we experience satisfaction and are stimulated to bear witness to mercy and faith. As a faithful religious, I no longer look on the poor in the same way. I do not help him only because of the feelings stirred in me, but I help him in order to fill his suffering heart, seeing in him Christ who dies. It is no longer the beauty of the body which attracts; it is compassion which unfolds.

There will be crises and steps backward, as there will be progress and victories over the ego. The resolve will grow while maintaining its fragility. One needs a strong identity to come out victorious.

> Our social and Church context is marked by a crisis of identities. There is great uncertainty about the identity of the religious and the priestly life, whereas there is little social demand that these identities be more significant and visible. In addition, there is a strong social pressure with regard to sexual and professional

identities, even if, because of the evolution of mores, and unemployment, these two fields are also marked by uncertainty. The resulting processes of identification, necessary to emotional maturity, are often rather chaotic. From there, one can come to focus exclusively on certain questions, like religious identity, sexual identity, professional identity (such and such ministry or field of study). These can become the center of all concerns. This context marks the brothers in formation.[48]

Formation will have to envisage a community climate which will first of all confirm emotional growth. It must also envisage personalized adjustments to be sure to allow for individual adaptation, according to the life experience of each candidate before his entry and according to his resistance. Flexibility during the period of formation will help to save vocations which at first sight may seem fragile and even lost. Times of regression, experiences out of the regular program can bring the person to be better reinstated later on into the regular life of the community.

Adaptation to studies

There was a time when intellectual formation was well planned and where those who entered the community found themselves in an environment in harmony with their formation. Times have changed. Now persons come to us with diverse educational and cultural backgrounds. Several of them received a vocational or scientific *à-la-carte* training with a multiplicity of choices. Introduction to studies requires programs adapted to the new generation and supposes that the intellectual formation is offered according to the needs of each one. Currently, in certain communities, insistence is placed on intellectual formation to the detriment of the development of practical aptitudes on pastoral or professional levels.

We have entered a period in history where the needs of formation will be extremely diverse according to the needs of different Christian communities and individuals. Admittedly, a basic intellectual formation must be assured. But is it necessary that this formation be given to everyone altogether at the same time? Programs and methods will have to be adapted to varying temperaments and aptitudes. They will have to answer to different professional requirements according to future personal and communal commitments. A little more creativity would facilitate this integration. Proposals for training courses or experiments lived out of the framework of studies could be suggested for certain candidates.

Moreover, an overly rigid teaching system runs the risk of excluding the less gifted from religious life. An adapted pedagogy would make it possible to open our doors to people bearing witness more through their holiness and less by their knowledge. Certain communities have already made efforts in this direction. But much still remains to be done so that religious life does not become a select club of "good thinkers." We still need saints like the Curé d'Ars. We need apostles to go and evangelize the poor. And who are best prepared to go if not those who have lived the same experience?

Our programs of studies are often flawed. They do not always offer introductory and initiation courses which could facilitate the training of those less gifted in the field. Hopefully, the example given by certain seminaries can be of help. Programs conceived for older candidates have been successfully set up in various places. Our religious communities could imitate them.

Conclusion

In conclusion, suffice it to say that the current situation invites us to become more inventive and open to new perspectives. Let us unite our efforts so that religious life becomes an environment where happiness is still possible. Especially, let us bluntly put the question: "Is there still a place for the poor in our communities?" If so, then we will really be evangelical signs. If not, we will become clubs of "the elite." In such a case, there are few chances that religious life will continue to exist for long.

PERSONS IN CHARGE OF FORMATION AND OF THE COMMUNITY OF FORMATION

Introduction

These last thirty-five years, numerous experiments have been undertaken to improve formation and its programs. Formerly, the persons in charge of formation, the candidates and the mentors formed a distinctive group, especially in novitiates and theological colleges. Contacts with the older members were reduced to a minimum. There was insistence on the repetition of the same gestures, prayers, and other things, to form a *"habitus"* in the young people. It was thought that by developing reflexes of regularity a personality was structured. Everyone was formed to community life amid people of the same generation on the basis of daily communal life. Living in daily proximity with others forged character and promoted adaptation. For a time, the formula was successful. Then, we came to sub-groups and later, to integration within the larger community, especially in apostolic congregations and orders. Certain communities were artificially created with personnel selected to act as a structure for the young religious. Inter-novitiates appeared later, where communities shared some resources for the benefit of a very small number of postulants or novices in each congregation, convent or monastery. Through all these experimentations, we gathered rich experiences and all involved could bring convincing and favorable arguments for each formula used.

It seems to me that there is no ideal regrouping for formation. Minimal conditions are to be foreseen for the supervision of postulants, novices or scholastics. Attitudes, behaviors, and environment can support the maturation and harmonious development of those in formation. A mentality has to be developed so that the formation bears fruit. The object of the reflections in this chapter is to deal with the persons in charge of formation and the community of formation.

The ideal community

The ideal community does not exist and never will. Moreover, if it ever existed, it would be a contradiction in terms. It would be an artificial community, outside a real context. A person is formed in a natural environment which has positive qualities and some deficiencies. Newcomers must be integrated into a community which is comprised of faults, weaknesses and also greatness. The newcomer will quickly have noticed what is not going well in the community. We can hope that the postulant or the beginner will find, in this community, imperfect people in search of a sense to their lives, and people with a normal and serene life path, seeing their existence in the peace of God. The "ideal community" is that which presents a human face corresponding to reality. This face must thus express features showing joy and peace, but also daily difficulties, including occasional suffering. By the practice of the vows and observance of a common life, this community should exhibit a sense of direction, a precise vision of what religious life is all about. Its orientations and its lifestyle must be coherent. The rule and the constitutions should not simply be reference books collecting dust on the shelves of our libraries. The mission must respect the charism proposed by the spirit of the founder as well as by today's needs.

Cases of scandal or bad conduct that show individuals in revolt or decline do not help the flowering of a formation community. Such situations do not invite the desire to embrace religious life. All the members of a community of formation must be impregnated with goodwill. One has to like what one has to do. The person who enters a community needs to feel that the task of community living is serious and is accepted by all. To like doing what one has to do is an indication of an interior disposition where, in spite of our differences and our defects in character, we are able to address ourselves to the task of personal conversion under the umbrella of fraternal friendship. Here, the common good takes precedence over the individual good. Narcissism, be it personal or collective, favors division and discord. Daily contact with difficult cases weakens those young people who enter our communities; and in the long run can discourage them. The multiplicity of problems and conflicts results in the depreciation of religious life and heightens distaste for common life. These situations initiate the loss of the original enthusiasm and invite apathy and mediocrity. Indifference settles in and the individual will overrides submission to the superiors and to the Gospel. The rule of life loses its significance. In our formation communities, without establishing a perfect community of elite members, there should be no psychopaths constantly obstructing a climate favorable to the development of healthy living practices.

A shared responsibility

We know well that the person in charge of formation plays only a partial role in formation. It is especially the community which is formative. It forges the context where vocations grow. Each one of its members becomes the model for those who will constitute the future. Theirs is a primary responsibility. When we are all aware of that the members become jointly responsible. If each one feels that he has a common mission along with the person in charge of formation, he will certainly be more attentive to control his personal behavior. He makes a mistake if he believes that the responsibility of formation falls solely on the shoulders of the person in charge of formation. Influence on others is always reciprocal. The postulants or novices will perpetuate the models which surround them. They will imitate the conduct and will follow the teachings of their elders. On the whole, the newcomers will be influenced by what they see and hear! Everything changes when we manage to persuade the members of the community that the religious in formation will do tomorrow what the elders do today. Many things can be modified if the brothers or sisters of the community believe in the formation. It is not necessary to be saints, but one must sense that the members want to become saints and are making intentional efforts towards that goal. The environment has to support emulation. Community solidarity is manifested at the level of observance. Friendship and conviviality take root in common practices which, when accepted by all, reinforce fraternal bonds. Common work also helps to develop solidarity with the mission. Without this solidarity, the mission becomes burdensome to carry and loses its effectiveness. Today's religious and priests are probably the most individualistic of our fellow-citizens. And they blame our modern society.

Today, how our candidates to religious life are adapting is often questioned. It seems to me that it is also necessary to question how the community is adapting to the newcomers. Higher ranking superiors have the responsibility to assign persons in charge of formation flexible enough to support the task of formation and those open enough to change their preconceived ideas while letting themselves be challenged by the younger generation. By a coherent institutional logic, the persons in charge of formation get the essential support of fellow-brothers and sisters who will agree to accommodate the younger generation with kindness and benevolence. Thus the young people will take their place and will avoid letting themselves being infantilized by an environment too paternalistic and too sure of itself.

Autonomous monastic communities are in a particular situation. It seems that several of them are no longer able to accommodate newcomers because of the ageing of its members. We already spoke about the possible regroupings for formation. In certain countries, experiments along this line have been successfully carried out. The inter-novitiates and the years of training lived in a well selected monastery of a Federation could allow the formation of communities capable of accommodating newcomers. Subsequently, these well trained people could currently belong to the monasteries that appear to be "running out of gas" as it were and having few chances of surviving.

Who has to adapt?

To adapt means "to bring oneself into harmony with" circumstances and environments. But it also means to be accustomed to living with people, in precise places and foreseen customs with which we are not always in agreement! This adaptation does not mean that we completely abandon what up till now was part of our past and the society where we come from. On the one hand, a person can have real difficulty integrating in a certain context; and, on the other hand, those who already live there see their world disturbed by the newcomer. It takes a lot of listening and understanding on both sides. A community refusing to renew itself through contact with new ideas is on the march towards its death. No community custom is guaranteed to be permanent. Throughout history, people have adjusted themselves to their own culture and to the culture of others. The beauty of life comes from perpetual renewal. It is a blessing that life changes little by little with the coming of new knowledge and ways of doing and of thinking.

"To accompany" means "to walk with" those whose life you share. Our traditions are important to them. They form part of our history and newcomers want to adhere to them by adopting them. That can however block a certain critique of the present. It seems to me that this, too, could become an obstacle to progress. Here is the "burden" about which the Gospel speaks. There is the impression, particularly for the people between forty and sixty-five years of age, that everything should be considered according to their particular universe. They wish that all those who enter might have the same ideas, passions, desires and hopes that they have. We forget the cultural distance between generations. What, then, is to be done?

Three months after I entered the novitiate, my master of novices said to me: "I can't understand how it is that you are still here. I never thought that you would persevere so long." After long years of experience as the person in charge of formation he was convinced that I did not have what was necessary to persevere. But it was my good luck to have had him as my master. He helped me by respecting me. As person in charge of formation, he accepted my differences, in spite of his doubts. I was of a certain age and I had had some worldly experience and a structured personality. He knew well that I would not change my personality at the age of forty-six. He respected all of us during the novitiate. He knew how to adapt his methods, and it was difficult for him. He himself had not received much formation as master of novices. However, he was a religious at heart. His enthusiasm gave him a certain authority and called for our respect.

The community is like a married couple. The birth of the first child changes the parents' lives. The practices of the couple can no longer be the same as before. Where before it was possible to accommodate their professional and married life with flexibility and freedom, in the fusion or in the interdependence of the couple, it will now be necessary to readjust and to take into account the newcomer. This individual has special needs; it will want to occupy all of the attention. The same will be true of the second child and the others to come. In our religious communities, we often have this bad habit of creating barriers to newcomers and their desires. Accustomed to a more or less regular life, we expect the newcomers to adjust to our rhythm of life and our ideas. We want to fit them into our universe. Their questions, their criticisms, their opinions end in frustrating our hope to perpetuate ourselves in them. With each new child, a family must readjust its behavior. The interpersonal relations will have to be adjusted to the new "deal." It is the same thing for a religious community. It is necessary to accept the inconveniences of the differences between generations.

Dialogue between the various generations is necessary. Newcomers have to learn, if they don't know it already, that the elders can bring them the fruit of their experience. For the elders, acquired knowledge and the experiences of life provide them with certain wisdom. The newcomer must sip this wisdom by listening with benevolence. He must agree to pace himself to the community and to become part of the ways of living of a group already made up and structured.

The elders who welcome them also have to become conscious that the group in its structure and its behavior is not eternal. The renewal of the group can only take place if this group accepts changing certain things. An amenable attitude of reception necessarily implies an experiencing of what is new and changing. To refuse would be equivalent to the slow death of the group. The wisdom of the elders must also put up with the naivety of the newcomers. By their youth or their inexperience, they open new prospects. It is necessary to bring something new to the community without disavowing the past.

The elders must respect the maturity and especially take into account the past lives of those who join them. Their experiences add new richness to the life of the group. That requires that the brothers already assigned in the communities of formation be capable of empathy. There is no place for a narcissistic spirit. Taking into account the other is fundamental.

The person in charge of formation

A person can be responsible for formation at any age, providing he has certain qualities. That can be surprising: the person in charge of formation has to be neither perfect nor holy. He is first and foremost the one who is the pilot of an authentic religious life. It is not holiness that makes the person in charge of formation successful, but rather his authenticity. Out of that, something good can come. Young people will be sensitive to the example of a humble and sincere person in charge of formation. Frankness plays a pacifying role in relationships even if the truth is often hard to hear. Frankness calms situations. Objectivity is essential in appeasing sensitivities.

The authority of the person in charge of formation must be recognized and respected by all. Otherwise, his role could easily be undermined. He could make errors of judgment out of fear of possible reactions to his decisions; to avoid this he must feel that he has a free hand. Those in formation want to know who they are dealing with. They will rely on the authority of the person in charge of formation only if the whole community, and especially major superiors, recognize it. A fundamental principle, one that is found in business management, has to be applied to the principle of authority in community. No one can be held accountable for situations if he does not have the appropriate authority to manage them. Responsibility requires the delegation of corresponding authority. Moreover, the line of authority should always be followed and the levels of responsibility should never be ignored. A provincial, an abbot, a prior should never bypass the master of formation to correct the situation of a religious under his responsibility.

Formation teams are often the cause of difficulties for the candidates in formation. How many efforts have been made un-productive because the responsibility for formation was assigned to several people? Who is at the helm? Who decides? Especially, who appreciates the situation? To whom will one entrust his concerns, with the assurance of discretion and a certain competence?

The setting of the person in charge of formation is the

community of formation. The candidate identifies himself with it as a religious. During the time of formation, the guide acts as a mentor and as a point of reference. Only the person in charge holds the reins and accompanies the candidates. He does not pilot the plane by consensus. Nor does he deal with the lives of those in formation by "committee," or by coded messages transmitted by others who have no authority. A council of formation is sufficient. Let the person in charge of formation do his job.

No one wants to have above himself several persons who have the right to judge and decide without the possibility of identifying and pointing out who is doing what. One person in charge of formation is enough! A candidate wishes to interact with a person, not with a team, a council, or a group. Things have to be clear. Those who take decisions must be accountable for what they say and do. Sometimes, individuals tend to hide behind institutional authorities (councils or committees) to avoid publicly expressing their own opinion for fear of being refuted or judged. If suggestions, recommendations or comments are to be made, they should not be hidden. It is essential to be able to take responsibility for one's judgment on a person or situation. Private matters should not be discussed at a council or at a team meeting without the person concerned having the possibility of justifying himself or at least of being informed. Councils of formation, designed to help the person in charge of formation better determine the motivations of each person, should not be closed or secret. If we don't want the person to know what we think, it is better to abstain from saying anything. Certain situations are better discussed only with the person in charge of formation and out of the councils.

It is good for the person in charge to have access to deputies or assistants who perform precise functions and whose roles are clear to all. In the Dominican Order, we have the custom of naming an assistant-master or *socius*. This is very wise! It makes it possible for the religious in formation to find an attentive ear to discuss problems that could pop up. The assistant-master can play a very positive role in conflictive situations. He can also wisely advise the person in charge of formation on this or that precise case.

It is also desirable to call upon external specialists for conferences or lectures on various topics. The person in charge of formation cannot be a specialist in everything. Especially during the novitiate, the lecturers play an important part in the objective presentation of the charism of the community or any other subjects in which they are qualified. However, the person in charge of formation must always retain the responsibility for accompanying individual candidates. Other people can be called upon to direct certain other activities. The theological colleges of yesteryears are now very few. But certain communities still have houses of study. The relationship between professors and those in charge of formation is always a work of collaboration in progress. An open relationship and mutual support can only be beneficial to the overall training of the religious. Formation is a totality and studies must go hand in hand with human and spiritual formation.

In many communities, formation in small groups is encouraged in order to get members used to life with a family character. Too large a group is likely to allow for a certain isolation and an invitation to individualism. If such a fear is justified, space must also be provided for a plurality of community situations. Those who enter a community that is too small may not be able to live daily side by side in a situation where character traits irritate and weaken one's development and formation. The number of religious must be sufficient to make it possible for the individual to find various personalities and different temperaments within the group. The persons responsible for the kitchen or for the laundry are important individuals who lighten the group's dynamics. They are often models to which one can point in discussing aspects of the religious life or its history. They teach by the testimony of their prayer and work. Along with the apostolic religious and the elders who form the community, they present the image of an interior stability that the newcomer needs to feel. Small communities can easily disappoint because their common life is often too demanding. Daily friction between the members can erode goodwill in a vocation where life with many confreres is not always easy. Small communities are also apt to abandon to loneliness the young candidates because of the external obligations of the members.

The relation between the person in charge of formation and the person in formation

It is preferable to have a person in charge of formation for each different phase of formation. In most communities, that does not cause any problem. However, in contemplative monasteries, there is a difficulty. Sometimes, the religious in formation have the same person in charge of them for six to eight years. Here is the danger. A change of those in charge of formation would be preferable following novitiate. The stages of formation would thus be better delineated and the personality of the person in charge with his specific talents could be better utilized according to the various stages. He could thus be selected according to the specific objectives of each phase.

In addition, it is necessary to avoid becoming too familiar with the candidates in formation. The person in charge is a confidant, but he runs the risk of knowing too much and not being impartial any longer. A legitimate friendship has its place because it allows confidence, dialogue and humor in the relationship. However, too much familiarity in the long run risks creating complicity and too much proximity and, with time, interferes with communication by distorting the relationship. And let us not think that only the female or contemplative communities have to deal with this situation! The relationship of a master who is a confidant on the one hand, with too much proximity on the other, risks degenerating into an inappropriately close one. It is important that those in charge of formation keep a certain distance.

Interpersonal conflicts can easily generate very strong antipathies if the relationship is too familiar. That can become unbearable for both parties. Sometimes sensitivity is likely to take the precedence over reason. Then, reprimands or suggestions take on unexpected proportions and can be interpreted as a rejection.

A too-prolonged subservient situation tends to favor a regression to the stage of childhood. A formation which does not correspond to the adult age of the candidate can lead to insubordination and psychological fatigue which produces certain tensions. The master then loses a sense of responsibility and no longer supports autonomy.

In many places, it seems we have kept in place a cycle of formation answering to now outdated situations. A formation that envisaged long stages because of very young candidates could be justified at one time. Today, candidates enter at a more advanced age and the stages should better correspond to adult stages of development. Our methods should be adapted to chronological age.

Each stage must have a particular aim. That of the novitiate should be a time when spiritual life takes precedence over apostolic life. It would be critical to skip this stage in which the future religious is meant to develop his skills in the spiritual life. Contemplation is situated in importance above an active life of work. A religious is not a skilled specialist who has only a tiny bit of time to devote to God and to the mystery of man. It is during his contemplative moments that the religious finds the necessary spiritual subsistence for his mission in a world culturally estranged to faith. Thus the accent placed on certain aspects of religious life varies according to the stages and the needs of the religious.

Religious culture

Many candidates lack a religious culture. However, we should nuance that. The religious culture we received was transmitted to us through various channels according to our age. Admittedly, catechism was inculcated in us at school. But we memorized notions by heart without internalizing them with full conviction. They were often assimilated without adhesion.

It seems to me that the postulancy is the best time to acquire religious knowledge. This presumes that the necessary time will be granted to the members in formation by including a program of education in the faith during that phase. It also provides an opportunity to involve other members of the community in formation. Some have the gift of teaching and others that of accompaniment.

Psychological accompaniment

Psychological accompaniment should never be handled by the person in charge or by another religious from the community. Moreover, two people of the same community should not be sent to the same professional at the same time. It is better that the psychologists be totally independent and not involve themselves in community matters. The community should not become a laboratory for research purposes. There have been some unhappy experiences in this respect. Psychological accompaniment is valid and one should not abstain from resorting to it. Ideally, it should be made before entrance into the community and never during the canonical novitiate unless it is truly urgent. Rather it should be made after profession if necessary.

Training those in charge of formation

"How do you see formation in your community, in your Federation?" This was the question I posed in a session with women persons in charge of formation in several contemplative monasteries. The answers were surprising and several proposals were advanced. Would it not be necessary to take the preparation of the persons in charge of formation more seriously? Admittedly, the experience of religious life – and of life itself for that matter – is necessary and valid. But difficulties met by persons in charge of formation today more than justify an adequate preparation. A formation given by specialists in that domain prepares the person in charge of formation and makes him or her feel secure at their task. The State and society allocate many human and didactic resources for the training of their personnel. Aren't the stakes just as important for us, religious?

Too often, persons in charge of formation have been deprived of a time of formation before taking up their task. Here, a wise precaution is essential in all justice for those who will come to share our life. Don't they have a right to the best mentors? The future of our communities depends on the training of its members. This formation plays a great part in the equilibrium of a person, and the prospect of duration in religious life likewise depends on it in large part. Those in charge of formation should not hesitate to follow courses in this field offered by various organizations. It is a question for the Church at large to face.

Hopes and fears

Religious expect a great deal from our formation programs. The length of this period is seen as an ideal model which will answer all the community's requirements and will guarantee perseverance. For the newcomer, to go through a formation program to the end is an achievement and the religious do not fail to admire those who succeed. Our masters of formation do not always appeal to today's vocation prospects. They are undoubtedly assigned to that task for their qualities, but these qualities are not necessarily those which newcomers would expect from them. Past parental experiences will influence the view which they will have of them. For many, the relationship will depend on an open attitude on the part of the person in charge. In spite of that, the master of formation can seem to be a threat. The differences of mentality between the generations will influence the credibility of the master vis-à-vis those who are entrusted to him or her. There is a certain fear of being manipulated by the person in charge. You can either bear with his or her leadership or be crushed by it. Often, this occurs on the unconscious level and remains in the domain of the unspoken.

The prospect of long years of studies does not facilitate a serene advancement in the face of the task of religious life. To study, as positive and necessary as it might be, is still to return to a state where a candidate may feel that he is regressing to childhood. Many adults find it difficult to go back to intellectual work. Subjected to the trends of sometimes very different and even conflictive public opinion, convictions are shaken. Intellectual work, so long emphasized in the Church, can trouble the consciences of those who have pursued different currents of thoughts. Because of a new vocabulary, the study of philosophy or theology sometimes upsets mentalities little accustomed to a critical spirit. The search for direction is confronted with the study of a more or less speculative reality. Whereas faith and prayer fostered the search for meaning, intellectual speculation now comes to jostle certainties, and to dethrone long-held beliefs. In certain faculties of theology, this phenomenon is called: "the beginners' theological shock."

Teachers, preachers and lecturers must be careful not to shock the spirits by too entrenched an attitude on this or that subject. No matter the leanings of the professor in the field of theological reflection and his personal religious or pastoral convictions, he must take care not to affirm too hastily what the Church itself is in the process of discussing. One can easily disturb the conscience of religious in formation, often new converts themselves, and be likely to make them lose their taste for religious life or the priesthood, if not for the Gospel itself. Often, the polemical tone employed in faculties of theology does not help to confirm young people in their desire to follow Christ. A certain mistrust of piety sometimes questions the very reasons behind the choice of one's vocation. Respect for the progress of each one would avoid unforeseen disappointments.

Moreover, topics discussed in which some confusion was sown and which upset the inexperienced understanding or consciences of newcomers have sometimes resurfaced fifteen or twenty years later. People have found themselves disappointed not to have followed their first intuitions. Where a more or less healthy sense of humor was used to help people evolve in the name of open-mindedness, consciences may have been wounded. Later, they may realize the fragility of their lives, their limits, and they will give up, for lack of fervor, which appeared perhaps naive, but which became their major conviction. How many religious left saying: "I don't believe in it any more!" A large number of religious were weakened in their faith by the lack of serious theological or spiritual reflection. How many behaviors became acceptable which at the time of initial formation would have been unacceptable? Serious responsibility falls on the shoulders of those in charge of formation. Each candidate must be given time to digest their reflections. They need to be invited to reflect in a climate of research absent of any hint of absolutism. Young people long for open-mindedness, but never apart from the Gospel. Sometimes we are astonished to see people asserting this or that with such assurance. Everything must be screened in light of the Gospel. The authoritative tone of an "omnipotent" Church on the intellectual level cannot lead to faith or to spiritual progress. Here, the humility of those in charge of formation will lead to dialogue and understanding.

This intellectual reflection must be done in a climate of prayer and charity. Humility must preside over our teaching.

"Let us give time to time." It is better to doubt our knowledge than to allow a pretentious attitude to settle in, which, under the pretext of humor, can wound consciences. A little humility can help one grow.

Conclusion

We can say that to be a person in charge of formation represents a grace for all those who have had that experience. They receive as much or more than they give. To welcome young or not so young people today is a chance to realize one's own potential for exercising a healthy paternity or maternity because all of these candidates are accepted in the name of Christ who said: "Come and follow me"; "You are my friends."

CHAPTER EIGHT

EVALUATION

Introduction

In our communities, the process of evaluation is often con-ducted without methodology. Not that we hesitate to formulate judgments or to engage in more or less relevant conversations. On the contrary, each and every one contributes with his grain of salt. No one hesitates to put ideas forward according to his intuitions. However evaluation is very important in the updat-ing of our systems of formation and a certain prudence is to be exerted in this field. It is thus necessary for us to take it seriously. There are two kinds of evaluations which should be done. The first relates to the training program, its repercussions on the life and the future of the community. The second kind touches the evolution of the person in formation, his progress as well as his setbacks, his realizations on the human and the spiritual levels.

Some general considerations

I do not think I'm mistaken when I say that each person in charge of formation should be considered accountable for his management. The person in charge of formation cannot be completely autonomous. One of his most delicate tasks is the account to be given about the people and their evolution. He carries their future in his hands. To a certain extent, the future of his community is also concerned. We have all been marked by the formation received and it has oriented our future behavior.

We propose clues which could help concerning the process. For most people, the evaluation is something threatening. We know that it is necessary. Then how do we make the process more human and more accessible to those who are the object of this process, as well as to those who perform it? The evaluation must be very simple, without fanfare. It must be perceived as an opening and not as a control. Listening is of the essence. It is necessary to want to hear, not to be closed to ideas, comments, or suggestions. This supposes that the person in charge of formation does not feel threatened by a given position or ideology; because one of the enemies of objective evaluation is the ideology which dictates the ideas of each member of the community, his future, his vision. Several factors are at play, among which the age of the person in charge of formation and that of the person whom he evaluates, the education he has received, and his hidden intentions. Those are often expressed by images which do not always correspond to reality. For the persons in charge of formation, the evaluation could become the means of advancing the unspoken comments and the accumulated frustrations in relation to what was lived. In this respect, one needs understanding and broad restraint to come to a conclusion about the program as well as about the people involved.

The candidate in formation

The evaluation of the candidate in formation consists of a day to day examination by the person in charge of the formation as well as by the person concerned. The one in charge is responsible for maintaining a climate of confidence with the religious in formation where he does not feel judged but supported in his advancement and encouraged to reflect on his progress as well as on his failures. This examination, then, becomes an occasion where the person feels affirmed, even loved. The religious in formation needs to know that he is wanted by the community and that those in charge of formation have confidence in him.

On this level, the evaluation is personal and confidential. At the time of the interview, one should not take any notes in view of constituting a file. It is a day to day evaluation. It is abstract, friendly, and affectionate. It can sometimes result in agreements, in simple and convivial language, on new objectives to be pursued. We are not a company. We are a community of brothers who appreciate and pursue together a path to holiness. There is no particular deadline to become a saint, since everything is in God's hands under the motion of the Holy Spirit.

This dialogue can be facilitated by raising points of interest: community life and relations with others, prayer life, conversation, *lectio divina*. The spiritual life is of prime importance, since it is where an individual's relationship with God is strengthened. A weakness in this respect can indicate a tendency to be scattered, and to have a lack of attention regarding essentials. It can be an indication of dissatisfaction compared to the enthusiasm identified at the time of entrance to the novitiate.

Community tasks and chores are activities where the person develops a sense of responsibility. It is in work that the rooting in the community is realized and verified. A lack of interest in this area can mean difficulty of integration, a lack of spirit at work or fragile health and certain apathy.

A discussion about the vows gives true indications on the candidate's adaptation to his choice of life. His relationship to authority makes it possible to assess in dialogue his capacity for adult obedience. Sensitivity can play a role in his response to requests and the requirements of daily life. It is an occasion to speak about family experiences which influence his relations with the authority. The vow of chastity, where the person is confronted with his emotions and emotional life, invites him to evaluate his connections with outside and family relationships. Is he capable of detachment on this subject? Do family and friends take so much space that they disturb too much his imagination and heart? Are particular friendships critical to the point of disturbing the individual and of being the cause of conflictive relations with fellow-members? Are they an impediment in the apostolate? This might be an occasion for detecting any experienced sufferings which could require a frank and respectful exchange. This dialogue gives an opportunity to support the commitment in which the candidate wants to be engaged and to find new supports to persevere in his effort to be chaste.

This would also be the moment to give an account, at the level of the vow of poverty, of expenditures and to check certain tendencies to the possession and accumulation of goods which blocks the freedom to openness. A particular apostolate and the community mission are like landmarks making it possible to check his interest in the mission in accordance with the charism of the community. Apostolates, as small as they might be during formation, are revealing indicators of the attachment to Christ and of the desire to serve others.

Evaluation

The evaluation is also the time to evoke the future, the hopes, the projects, the tastes, the prospects vis-à-vis the apostolate and future work. The idea of the religious life in general differs from one person to another. The evaluation makes it possible to assess the appropriation of fundamental elements of religious life, of the insertion in a project connected with the Church.

Other points can be approached according to the seasons of life. Each one can find matters to discuss. No subject must be taboo or rejected. All is valid. All must be taken seriously by the person in charge of formation. Only the religious in formation counts, as well as what he is living.

The candidate must understand that all that is said is said under confidentiality. Here, it is necessary to distinguish well between the intimate conscience and external behavior. The person in charge of formation will often be exposed to receiving confidences in the realm of an individual's intimate conscience. He must treat them accordingly. Those things should never be revealed. Each one has a right to his privacy and nobody has the right to make use of it to pass judgment. However, what the person in charge of formation learns from other sources or what he observes can and sometimes must be revealed to the superiors, if the good of the community or that of the candidate is concerned. We will come back to this matter later in relation to the report submitted to the community and the superiors. The community council does not have any right to know what is said in private interviews with the candidates. Nor do the superiors either. The rule of discretion is the best guarantee of maintaining a climate of confidence. The question will arise of knowing on which criteria the community, the council and the superiors have to judge.

The reports of psychologists and other experts cannot be revealed to anyone in the community without the consent of the concerned person acting freely and without any compulsion. Personally, I do not ask any psychologist to give me a report regarding the situation of somebody whom I would have proposed for therapy. Besides, I am always astonished at the facility with which information on the capabilities of an individual for religious life is revealed following a psychological test. I am against this form of investigation. It is very strange how these methods of discernment developed in the Church. There are other means to discover if somebody has the necessary aptitudes. It is the role of pre-formation to envisage periods of normal observation related to any commitment in a community. In case of doubt, the person in charge of formation can suggest to a candidate that he submit himself to a consultation to better distinguish his vocation. But then the result should remain confidential.

This being said, I do not hesitate to entrust to a psychologist any person who could need some consultation. Simple conversations, accompanied by suitable questions like: "You spoke to your therapist about it?" easily elicits what the psychologist thinks. If not, it is perhaps because the psychologist did not judge it appropriate to address the question. Rare are the candidates who do not have the goodwill to exchange freely. They are often afraid of psychotherapy for fear of indiscretions. Too close a bond between the psychologist and the superiors could put the exchanges and confidences at risk. It is necessary to dissociate the function of the professional from that that of the mentor and the superior.

The evaluation report to the community and the council

The report for acceptance by the community must be submitted on the basis of objective and observable facts regarding behavior.

Affectivity can be mentioned only if external behavior indicates a problem at this level.

Here are useful points to treat with the community:

- intellectual life, the effort to study reveals the aptitude for an activity of reflection necessary to all religious. Some will be less gifted, others more capable. A lack of interest does not bring into question the vocation. But the difficulties will determine the pedagogy and the investment necessary to arrive at a sufficient knowledge. An over-investment could underline a tendency to escape from reality;

- relationships with others reveal emotional difficulties, charitable desires, the aptitude for living with others. Often, relationships reveal if one is happy or not;

- assiduity shows the capacity for discipline; collaboration with others prevents individualism; concern about the common good allows for better control of selfishness; participation in the community project indicates an openness without narcissism. These ways of acting are many aspects of conduct which the candidate and the person in charge of formation can use to evaluate the capacity for living in a group;

- obedience to an authority is fundamental in religious life. It allows one to change the focus from oneself and makes it possible to better reflect with the superior about the stakes involved in community and apostolic life. It is one of the most adequate means to evaluate insertion in the life and the charism of the organization. Abnegation plays a particular part there;

- the religious embarks on the route of poverty. Is he able to live dependent on others or does he need total autonomy? Can he be satisfied with the minimum? Does he have a constant need to accumulate goods and creature comforts?

- missionary spirit and devotion are outstanding signs of service to others and the Church; verifying this spirit allows us to be confident that the individual has a true motivation in his vocation;

- an awakening to the needs of the Church and the environment shows the capacity to judge. Good judgment is fundamental in the exercise of charity in the Church. It is the necessary fundamental attitude for making progress and advancing on the road to sanctity. The efficiency of the mission and the quality of life depend on a sound judgment;
- participation in community prayer verifies the effort to overcome any tendency to indolence and the capacity to persevere in an institutionalized life. It is an indicator of the depth of one's relationship with God and others;
- it is by the joys and the sorrows expressed outwardly that the motivation to be a religious is discovered. By these signs, one can distinguish the will to persist in a state of life where one must face day to day reality.

Once the community and the superiors are informed, they are ready to pass judgment and can communicate their points of view. As has been seen, the matters to be discussed relate to external behavior. The observations can be noted and then revealed to the candidate without identifying those who reported them. However, the comments should be revealed. Those who do not want their comments to be known should rather abstain from making any. What is known can leave wounds. Words and their consequence have to be measured. The absence of judgment or understanding on the part of one or another should not be revealed. These community evaluations don't have to be very frequent; once a year seems sufficient to me.

Then the Council can itself evaluate what was said in the community and assess the relevance of the judgments made, but always under the same rule of discretion. In what concerns the conscience, it is judicious to invite the religious in formation himself to make a decision regarding his vocation rather than the community having to take it. In any case, if the problem is serious, the person will be brought to decide himself about his departure.

An evaluation of the programs

Every four or five years, it is good that the Chapters consider the formation programs. This evaluation does not include a rule of discretion, since only the programs are being discussed. However, a practical method which does not confuse things ought to be used. Questionnaires made up of precise and objective points can lead to serious reflection regarding the stages of formation. Each question must be weighed and reflected upon. It is useful to check and validate these questions through follow-up questions in order to determine more precisely the problems and to discuss pertinent and verifiable points. Often, sensitivity leads the exercise to get lost in matters that are not very important or with little interest. Closed or open-ended questions also make it possible to check the reliability of the answers.

A convivial meeting can attract interesting suggestions. Problems should be discussed without exaggeration. It is necessary to find alternate solutions without wanting to transform everything. Constant changes, owing more to personal sensitivity than to a certain objectivity, disturb the process of formation and do not allow building in an uninterrupted way. Strongly held ideas often give way to arguments revealing dissatisfactions that are not all that serious. Experience and objective evaluation open the way to practical and coherent solutions. Ideologies die hard. To build the future, it is necessary to stick to experience.

This type of evaluation functions well if the objectives of formation are clear and known to the concerned parties. Each course, each method, each control must be the object of an evaluation within a more or less short time. Within the community, there should be at hand a religious qualified and informed regarding the various methods that can be used to evaluate the programs. The evaluation must always be made on the basis of the aims intended by the "*Ratio Formationis*" and by the decisions of the Chapters on formation. The intended aims put forward by the Church for clerics and religious must also be taken into account.

Religious in formation should be able to take part in the evaluation of the programs. In the process of living the experience of their formation, they can bring to religious life very relevant suggestions. All must be done in charity and especially in humility. No system is perfect and no formation is perfect. The important thing is to detect what supports a positive evolution of the programs and the people.

CHAPTER NINE

PASTORAL WORK WITH VOCATIONS

The Mysterious Choices of God Exerted on Men

At the center of the ups and downs of history, God seems to have judged wisely to choose His collaborators from different backgrounds. We see Jesus selecting some of His apostles from among very simple people. Others will be people having very precise functions in Jewish society. Some are "sinners"; others, "fishermen."

Curiously, since 1960, the legitimate desire to see educated, balanced and qualified clergy and religious, professionally as well as spiritually, limited the recruitment of religious and priestly vocations to those endowed with higher intellectual and human qualities, found only in certain environments. Old seminaries or juniorates had the utility and the interest of preparing people from all social backgrounds, especially those coming from the workplace or rural worlds. Now, vocations no longer come from poorer areas, for lack of pastors and religious really able to understand their mentality, to call them from where they are, and especially to prepare them for a commitment in the Church.

Let us follow the example of Jesus in our choice of vocations.

For his apostles, our Lord looked for poor, simple, ignorant, rustic and not so clever fishermen. He wanted to preach only for a few years and then go back to heaven after his resurrection. It was necessary to round up disciples to teach them his doctrine in order that, after His Resurrection, they might preach to Jews and Gentiles alike. They were to preach to all the inhabitants of the earth; therefore, it was necessary to find among them architects, workmen, and masons to build this very noble temple, this Church of all nations.

It was necessary to construct new heavens to sing God's glory. Finally, it was necessary to call Doctors and Founders of the Church who would teach the whole world, its people, princes, kings, and philosophers, the learned, the ignorant, and those who would establish the Church around the globe on people gathered as beautiful and precious stones who would form the foundation of the Holy Jerusalem.

Where does Our Lord go to find them? Did he go to Athens, fountain of philosophy, to Rome the mother of eloquence, to Jerusalem, city where the true wisdom was taught? No. He went to none of these large and superb academic sites to take from them doctors, philosophers, speakers like Cicero, Demosthenes, Aristotle, and Plato; rather he went to the Sea of Galilee to choose fishermen, poor people who did not have anything. Oh, Kindness of God! Oh Power! Oh Providence! Oh Wisdom! So that it might be for us an example and consolation, Our Lord called rough and unpolished men, and made fishers of men out of them.[49]

Are we ready to do as Our Lord did? Are we ready to go to the byways of this world and, through various means, challenge those whom we meet? Are we ready to work side by side in the Church with people of all conditions and more or less good formation?

What does the expression "pastoral care of vocations" mean if not the idea of approaching all kinds of people and bringing them to follow Jesus? The picture of the "Good Shepherd" can provide us with a new orientation. Do we want to become "shepherds"? To enter the dynamics of pastoral work with vocations, it is first necessary to be concerned about the future of the Church and the coming of the Kingdom, just *as a shepherd would*. We will not be able to communicate our enthusiasm unless we are ourselves convinced of the logic of an effective and urgent action to propose to today's world. The Good Shepherd is concerned about His sheep. He takes every means to ensure their safety and to nourish them. Are we true shepherds walking with our flock, or are we well fed individuals who are satisfied with what we have, letting the sheep go adrift? The first step in the "pastoral care of vocations" consists in changing how we speak about religious life. We may have conducted many analyses of the present situation and think we have grasped pretty well the difficulties we will meet today. But do we have the will to propose, to those who seek God and want to serve Him, a way towards the future?

Developing a Positive Attitude towards our Way of Life

To attract vocations, it is first necessary to believe in our own personal vocation and in the charism of our community. The first mediator to motivate someone to follow Jesus is the individual who has personally met Him in his own life. It is that person who is able to communicate the joy he has found in following Him. Happiness is self-communicative.

Criticism gives birth to suspicion. Why would we want to imitate anyone who is dissatisfied, who is constantly manifesting his frustrations? Individuals who hardly practice their religious life cannot communicate the desire to imitate them. Discouragements, pessimism, lack of openness to new generations, are factors which block the development of our communities. Through them, we give a false image of the religious life. Before proposing religious life, it might be useful to make a list of everything that is beautiful and good in our community and our life. We must show a positive attitude vis-à-vis religious life. It is necessary to have the thirst to live it and to get our teeth into it so to speak. To communicate it, it is necessary to capture its identity, its originality.

It is also necessary to present the new generation with a vision of the future for tomorrow's religious communities. This is particularly important for women's congregations. Who will be tomorrow's nuns? In examining this question, we have to consider the practices, intellectual development, motivations, and culture of the women of our time. We must be able to articulate religious life with a feminine vision in an understandable way for the 21st century woman. What will encourage a 25-year-old woman to follow Jesus? What type of religious life does she want to live? Some surveys provide hints for those responsible for formation: the strong desire in young people for prayer and fraternity, the need for a symbolic life (with signs pointing a way to the sacred), a universal vision of the future in a globalized culture; all are factors at play in the decision of a potential candidate. A mission rooted in the religious history of the people with an opening to modernity justifies a commitment. Upcoming generations choosing religious life must find coherence between the evangelical message and the mission toward humanity. They must find continuity between the history of a community, the founding rule of life, and the practices of the current group. We cannot propose a way of life which contradicts or which ignores the founding texts and the rule of life.

A visible community

We have to be visible if we are going to attract vocations. No one can desire what he does not see. Religious life is an institutional life made up of a group of people who like to be together, who have a common aim, a lifestyle and a manner of being and of working that is distinctive. Such a community makes the charism of the Congregation clear and palpable. The community cannot be a juxtaposition of individuals who, starting from a particular principle, follow a form of life under the direction of a guru. In this case it would be a sect. The success of the newer communities is due to their great visibility bolstered by a community life with an obvious fraternal spirit, a clear vision of their goals, and a radical choice of the Gospel and of the person of Jesus. They favor warmth, beauty in song and liturgy, and an attachment to the person of the Pope and to the Church.

The community must be the gathering of persons who openly choose Christ. It is faith in God and in the person of Christ that gathers them and not an idea. This person is the Son of God who died for our sins and is present by His Spirit for our salvation. He left us with an objective will: that of a way of life which can transform us and make us happy. The first means of attracting others is the enthusiasm of a community for Christ, Lord of the Harvest and Savior of humanity. He died and rose again for our salvation. He is always alive. We do not follow Jesus only because we admire Him so as we might follow some wise guru. He is the one who binds us together; He is the one to whom we are committed. Along with Him, we want to save the world. That must be reflected in our way of life and must be embraced with passion. If we follow Him, it is because we are convinced that it is necessary to continue the work of conversion begun in us, enlivened by His teaching and His preaching. Like Him, we want to lead the world to His Father. We cling to Him. In following Him, we do not lose our freedom. We freely commit our life through love of God and humanity. This is why we are not a sect. In a religious sect, an individual loses his freedom.

Religious need to be seen praying together. The prayer of a community must stir the desire to join it. People need to see a community sharing meals, and to discover in their midst a certain joy in living. They need to see religious helping one another, working in a common mission, having the same aspirations. They need to see the freedom of religious life. Religious life must propose something clear and different from what lay people live. Certain devoted individuals have a vocation to remain close to the world and to be present there. But religious life, while being related to the world around it, must remain an enclave where each and everyone can come and find a fraternity of prayer, sharing, and peace. It is often friendship with the group that stirs a desire to join it.

An open community

The topic of insertion of Religious in the world is often talked about. The opposition that was concocted between "the community" and "the world" came from an era of community life where many monks were less visible, generally residing in institutions. Moreover, not only were they encouraged to remain at their posts in the apostolate and to stay away from the world, but outsiders were invited to keep their distance as well. This was especially true of monastic life, though some apostolic communities were likewise reclusive. Often these communities had an institutional mission: schools, hospitals or other internal apostolates. In reaction to this tendency, communities were born at the dawn of the 20th century where insertion in the world was encouraged. Life in smaller groups was then necessary to allow this integration. Secular institutes and societies of apostolic life were established to answer a desire for greater closeness to the social milieu in which people lived. These new forms of consecrated life developed at a time when the apostolate of the laity was confined to rather passive roles, under the dependence of the clerics or monks.

Since the 1960s, things have changed. Religious hardly work anymore in their institutions. They have become "invisible," but in particular, they have formed small groups where their situation is often akin to lay status. Admittedly their houses are open, but for those whom they know well. They are known only in their immediate environment. They no longer form a visible entity with accessible means of welcoming.

As a result we notice a confusion of language in relation to religious life. The expression "consecrated life" includes several types of different commitments in the life of the Church. It is very difficult for people to easily recognize and identify exactly what a Religious is. It is not our intention here to solve what appears to us to be an identity problem for religious life. But it is nonetheless desirable that Religious strive harder than ever so that their community might be open to the greatest number of people in order to be better known and to make their vocation more accessible. If I might wish to join, it is necessary for me to see. Lay people need to be welcomed so that they can familiarize themselves with a way of life very different from their own. This openness can be very demanding when a Religious lives in a small group, because it asks for an investment of time and energy on the part of each member. Not everyone is always willing to welcome someone little known to them. We are in charge of souls; we are professionally committed to serve them, and thus we carry certain responsibilities. In these circumstances, we are constantly exposed to the public. Is it then necessary to accommodate each and everyone in our communities? Don't we need this time to pray, to rest, to live together? This is a legitimate question.

An external professional commitment is seen in society as employment. It is the person, not the community, who is present to the world. It is the Church at work in a setting that is, through me, putting my person at the service of the mission. So, for a community to be identifiable and understandable, it must show its face. This face of the community is visible today only through participation in its life, with its dynamics. Admittedly it is necessary to manage times and places where visitors will be welcomed, but that difficulty need not be an obstacle to doing something new to make our life better known. Religious are not expected to be committed like lay people; otherwise, it would have been better for many of them to stay in the world as lay persons! Why try to assimilate back into that which we initially left?

Here, we are confronted with the dynamics of the "not of the world and yet in the world."

Praying Communities

Today, we need to see Religious at prayer. Formerly, they gave testimony through their action, their apostolic work, their teaching or their involvement in health care. All these tasks have now been assumed in a more or less adequate way by very qualified and devoted personnel hired by the State in most developed countries.

The commitment of Religious was proverbial. You could always count on them. Everyone knew that they were available and ready for anything. Today, commitment is more general. *"Doctors without borders," "Restaurants of the heart,"* health care clinics, research labs, *Emmaus House*, the *Catholic Worker Movement*, the *Little Brothers of the Poor*, accommodations for persons "without permanent residence," soup kitchens, the *Red Cross*, etc. are all places where charity and commitment are practiced. Religious no longer have the monopoly on humanitarian organizations.

If Religious must still be present everywhere where there is a need, their action must give witness to their specific character. Their vocation now is to Christianize a secular world that promotes many excellent values, but which is lacking in meaning and is in search of spirituality. Increasingly, religious will have the vocation of bringing joy to others by their presence and their prayer. But this presence must be specifically Christian. Through their prayers of petition, praise, and contemplation they bring the world and its needs to God. They commend it into His hands.

An important gift that they bring to today's society is a sense of the meaning of life and they do so very effectively through the liturgy. We live in a world thirsting for spirituality and meaning. The prayer of a religious community should always be public, accessible to the people of the neighborhood. The poor will thus find a place where they can learn how to pray. The religious must pray with and for the Church. The Church is not only its structure and its institutions. Church life exists in, with and for persons. For us, it is necessary to pray, reflect, and share the Gospel. Big or small, communities should indicate those places and times when they will be at prayer, expressing their openness and willingness to accommodate those who are thirsty for God.

Take time to live

We live in a world where it is said, time is money. That confers on time a financial, material value. Time is a standard of effectiveness. It is an invaluable asset which should be used for profit. Time should be managed, given that its weight is in gold. The consequence of this view is that the individual is left with little time for himself. However, in the past people never enjoyed as many holidays, vacation days, and leisure time as they do today. "We don't see the time any more." We lose the notion of time because of the rapidity of communications, information, and the ease of transportation.

In religious communities, this new way of living has influenced our way of considering community life and mission. Our schedules are divided and regulated by our professional life, by television, by leisure hours and by a certain autonomy of action. For the apostolic religious there is thus a lack of time to do everything. Formerly, activities were regulated by religious practices and community exercises, thus it was more wisely controlled. Today, each one manages his own time, his own schedule. The speed with which we work, and the multiple activities we engage in keeps us very busy.

To newcomers, religious life must offer time to live differently. It is not the quantity of activities which makes the Gospel known. It is the human being who opens himself through faith in Christ and who takes time to be with Him. Attracting vocations takes time – to share, to live the common life. Young people need to find themselves in a community and it is this that attracts them. They need to pray, to reflect, to reveal themselves, to be involved in a project which draws their attention and devotion.

Our communities should offer a milieu where each one has time for himself and for others. It must take time for the Lord. Otherwise, it is not worthy of its calling. Secular society offers all that it is necessary to keep someone occupied. To offer time is to offer more than money. It is to offer a treasure that can be spent on study, prayer and fraternity. The mission comes in addition to complete the joy of living together.

This supposes that young people see us living in a balanced manner. This requires that we engage them in our mission, sharing our work with them. Volunteerism is an excellent way for them to experience and appreciate our charism. The employer-employee relationship will hardly bring vocations. We need to work with them on another level.

Conclusion

To truly engage in the pastoral work of vocations, it seems to me that it is necessary to propose a way of life without hesitating to put it forward. Publicity, means of communication, Internet, meetings, proposals of "*Come and see,*" along with many other things must be supported by our enthusiasm and a constant effort to make ourselves known. Christ approached the Apostles. He invited them. Let us not be afraid!

BIBLIOGRAPHY

Actes du chapitre général des prieurs provinciaux de l'Ordre des Prêcheurs, Bologne, 1998, n° 86.1.

JEAN-LOUIS BRUGUÈS, O.P., *L'éternité si proche. Conférences de Carême Notre-Dame,* Cerf, 1995, p. 31.

MICHELINE D'ALLAIRE, *Vingt ans de crise chez les religieuses du Québec,* Éditions Bergeron, 1983.

BERNARD DUCRUET, O.S.B., *L'obéissance retrouvée,* Pneumathèque, Société des œuvres communautaires, «Petits Traités Spirituels», 1997, p. 56.

CLAUDE GEFFRÉ, O.P., *Un espace pour Dieu,* Cerf, 1970, pp. 32-33.

GROUPE DE RÉFLEXION DE L'INSTITUT DE PASTORALE DES DOMINICAINS, «Les réaménagements pastoraux: où en sommes-nous et où allons-nous?», *Église canadienne,* volume 33, n° 9, septembre 2000.

PHILIPPE MADRE, *L'Appel de Dieu. Discernement d'une vocation,* Éditions des Béatitudes, 1991.

TIMOTHY RADCLIFFE, O.P., Maître de l'Ordre des Prêcheurs, *Conférence lors de la seconde assemblée des Sœurs Dominicaines Internationales à Rome, du 9 au 12 mai 1998.*

_____ Maître de l'Ordre des Prêcheurs, «L'ours et la moniale. Le sens de la vie religieuse aujourd'hui, Conférence aux supérieurs majeurs de France», *La Documentation Catholique,* 7 mars 1999, n° 2199.

_____ Maître de l'Ordre des Prêcheurs, *Lettre à l'Ordre, avril*

1998, *La promesse de vie,* Information Dominicaine internationale (IDI).

_____ Maître de l'Ordre des Prêcheurs, *Je vous appelle mes amis,* Entretiens avec Guillaume Goubert, Paris, La Croix-Cerf, 2000; *I Call You Friends*, Ignatius Press, 2004.

ADRIENNE VON SPEYR, *Choisir un état de vie,* Namur, Culture et Vérité, 1994.

J.-M. ROGER TILLARD, O.P., *Devant Dieu et pour le monde. Le projet religieux,* Paris, Cerf, coll. «Cogitatio Fidei», 1974.

CARDINAL JEAN-CLAUDE TURCOTTE, *L'Église de Montréal,* 27 mai 1999, n° 20.

ENDNOTES

1 Laurent-Marie Pocquet du Haut-Jussé, *La vie religieuse d'après Saint Thomas d'Aquin* [Religious Life According to Saint Thomas Aquinas], Téqui ed., 1999, p. 37.

2 Friar Timothy Radcliffe, O.P., *Conférence lors de la seconde assemblée des Sœurs Dominicaines Internationales à Rome* [Master of the Order of Preachers, Lecture for the Second Assembly of Dominican Sisters, at Rome], May 9-12, 1998.

3 Claude Geffré, O.P., *Un espace pour Dieu* [A space for God], Cerf, 1970, pp. 32-33.

4 Adrienne von Speyr, *Choisir un état de vie* [Choosing a State in Life], Namur, Culture et Vérité, 1994, p. 5.

5 Ibid., p. 15.

6 J.M.R. Tillard, O.P., *Devant Dieu et pour le monde. Le projet religieux,* Paris, Cerf, coll. "Cogito Fidei," 1974, p. 62.

7 Ibid., p. 16.

8 Genesis 12:1.

9 Genesis 2:24.

10 Genesis 2:24, TOB footnote: "In verse 24 the author is ratifying the mutual attraction of men and women. They live together and form a unity; the new bonds reveal themselves to the stronger than the one linking them to their respective kinsmen."

11 Luke 14:25-26.

12 Philippe Madre, *L'Appel de Dieu. Discernement d'une vocation,* [God's Call. Discernment of a vocation], Ed. des Béatitudes, 1991, p. 27: "Souvent, dans la perception d'un appel, le Seigneur nous fait pressentir quelque chose; il nous suggère une amorce de direction à prendre. Mais on ne sait pas tout par avance, on ignore jusqu'où ce voyage va nous mener et quelles seront ses étapes ou ses méandres."

13 Exodus 3:11.

14 Acts 8:26.

[15] Acts 9:6ff.

[16] J.M. Roger Tillard, O.P., *Devant Dieu et pour le Monde. Le projet religieux*, Paris, Cerf, coll. "Cogitation Fidei," 1974, p. 67.

[17] Timothy Radcliffe, O.P., Master of the Order of Preachers, "The Bear and the Nun. The meaning of Religious Life today, conference to the Major Superior of France," *La Documentation Catholique*, March 7th 1999, no. 2199, p. 228.

[18] 1 Corinthians 9:19-23.

[19] 1 Corinthians 9:24-27.

[20] Reflection Group of the Dominican Pastoral Institute (Montreal), "Pastoral re-arrangements: What phase are we in, and where are we heading?" *Eglise canadienne*, Volume 33, number 9, September 2000, pp. 262-263: "In approaching young generations, it will prove useful to get acquainted with current research on their culture and search for meaning. Some traits emerge and should be taken into account: their sense of the precariousness of relationships and work; their sensitiveness to self-expression more than to tasks; their ignorance about various Christian traditions, their interest in other ancient religious traditions; etc. It seems that spiritual movements and networks stand a better chance of reaching them than parishes as such."

[21] Timothy Radcliffe, O.P., *The Bear and the Nun* […], p. 233.

[22] Ibid., p. 233.

[23] From the Roman Congregation of Saint Dominic, "But one must not be rushed" or "There is no urgency."

[24] Mark 10:29-30: "Jesus said to him, 'Truly I tell you, no one will leave home, brothers, sisters, mother, father, family or land for my sake and the Gospel's, without receiving a hundredfold now, in this time, in homes, brothers, sisters, mothers, children and lands, along with persecutions, and everlasting life in the world to come.'"

[25] St. Marcellin Champagnat, Founder of the Marist Brothers.

[26] Card. Jean-Claude Turcotte, L'Église de Montréal, 27 mai 1999, N° 20.

[27] Timothy Radcliffe, O.P., Maître général de l'Ordre des Prêcheurs, *Lettre aux jeunes en formation*.

[28] Philippe Madre, *L'appel de Dieu. Discernement d'une vocation*, Éditions des Béatitudes, 1991.

[29] Ibid., p. 58.

[30] Ibid., p. 67.

[31] Canon Law language uses the word "lay" in the sense of non-priest. Daily language uses this word to point to any person who has no religious or sacerdotal commitments.

[32] John 14:10c-11.

[33] Adrienne von Speyr, *Choisir un état de vie*, Namur, Culture et Vérité, 1994, p. 43.

Endnotess

[34] Jean Vanier, *La communauté, lieu du pardon et de la fête*, Montréal, Bellarmin, 1979.

[35] Frère Roger Paquet, O.P., member of the St. Dominic's Province of Canada.

[36] Micheline D'Allaire, *20 ans de crise chez les religieuses du Québec (1960-1980)*, Éditions Bergeron, 1983.

[37] Adrienne von Speyr, *op. cit.*, p. 84.

[38] Ibid., p. 52.

[39] Ibid., p. 53.

[40] Matthew 11:28-30.

[41] Philippians 3:13-16.

[42] Bernard Ducruet, O.S.B., *L'obéissance retrouvée*, Pneumathèque, Société des œuvres communautaires, "Petits Traités Spirituels", 1997, p. 56.

[43] Adrienne von Speyr, *op. cit.*, p. 63.

[44] *Actes du chapitre général des prieurs provinciaux de l'Ordre des Prêcheurs*, Bologne, 1998, n° 86.1, p. 44.

[45] Ibid., p. 44.

[46] Timothy Radcliffe, O.P., Maître de l'Ordre des Prêcheurs, *Lettre à l'Ordre, avril 1998, La promesse de vie*, Information Dominicaine internationale (IDI), p. 87.

[47] *Actes du chapitre général des prieurs provinciaux de l'Ordre des Prêcheurs, op. cit.*, p. 44.

[48] Ibid., pp. 45-46.

[49] S. Pierre Fourier (XVIIe s.), *Opuscules*, p. 481.

ST PAULS

This book was produced by ST PAULS/Alba House, the Society of St. Paul, an international religious congregation of priests and brothers dedicated to serving the Church through the communications media.

For information regarding this and associated ministries of the Pauline Family of Congregations, write to the Vocation Director, Society of St. Paul, 2187 Victory Blvd., Staten Island, New York 10314-6603. Phone (718) 982-5709; or E-mail: vocation@stpauls.us or check our internet site, www.vocationoffice.org